Spray Finishing
and Other Techniques

Spray Finishing
and Other Techniques

The Editors of
Fine Woodworking

The Taunton Press

T The Taunton Press
Inspiration for hands-on living®

The Taunton Press, Inc., 63 South Main Street, PO Box 5506, Newtown, CT 06470-5506
e-mail: tp@taunton.com

Jacket/Cover design: Susan Fazekas
Interior design: Susan Fazekas
Layout: Cathy Cassidy
Front Cover Photographer: Susan Lawson Jewitt, © The Taunton Press, Inc.
Back Cover Photographers: (clockwise from top left) Anatole Burkin, © The Taunton Press, Inc.; Mark Schofield, © The Taunton Press, Inc.; William Duckworth, © The Taunton Press, Inc.

The New Best of Fine Woodworking® is a trademark of The Taunton Press, Inc., registered in the U.S. Patent and Trademark Office.

Library of Congress Cataloging-in-Publication Data
Spray finishing and other techniques / the editors of Fine woodworking.
    p. cm. -- (The new best of fine woodworking)
  ISBN-13: 978-1-56158-829-9
  ISBN-10: 1-56158-829-6
 1. Wood finishing. 2. Spray painting. I. Fine woodworking. II. Series.
 TT325.S63 2005
  684'.084--dc22

2005019825

Printed in the United States of America
10 9 8 7 6 5 4 3 2 1

OCT 0 5 2006

The following manufacturers/names appearing in *Spray Finishing and Other Techniques* are trademarks: 3M® Acryl-Blue Glazing Putty, 3M® 2K Lightweight Putty, 3M Finesse-It®, ALLPRO® Spray Clear Acrylic, Ametek Lamb Electric Co.®, Apollo® 700, Behr®, Binks®, Bondo®, Campbell Hausfeld® HV 3000, Clorox®, Compliant Spray Systems Enduro Wat-R-Base® Poly Overprint, DAP®, Deft®, Delta®, DeVilbiss®, Eclectic Products Famowood® Super Lac, Fantastik®, General®, Grainger℠, Homestead Finishing Products TransTint®, Hydrocote® Resisthane Pre-Catalyzed Lacquer, J.E. Moser®, Cool-Lac, Klingspor®, Krylon®, Mapa® Glove, Masonite®, Meguiar's®, Milwaukee®, Minwax®, Minwax® Polycrylic, Mirka Abralon®, PAM®, Penetrol®, Plasti-Kote®, Powermatic®, Pratt & Lambert #38®, Rust-Oleum®, Sherwin-Williams® Kem Aqua, Sherwin-Williams Krylon™, Target® Coatings Ultra-Seal, Target® Enterprises Oxford Hybrid Gloss Varnish, Teflon®, Wagner®, Wagner® 2600, Watco®, Water Master® Clear Acrylic, Windex®, White Knight™, Zar®, Zinsser® Bulls Eye®, Zinsser BIN®

Working wood is inherently dangerous. Using hand or power tools improperly or ignoring safety practices can lead to permanent injury or even death. Don't try to perform operations you learn about here (or elsewhere) unless you're certain they are safe for you. If something about an operation doesn't feel right, don't do it. Look for another way. We want you to enjoy the craft, so please keep safety foremost in your mind whenever you're in the shop.

Acknowledgments

Special thanks to the authors, editors, art directors, copy editors, and other staff members of *Fine Woodworking* who contributed to the development of the articles in this book.

Contents

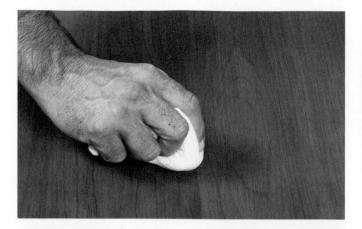

Introduction

My first experience with finishing furniture was typical of most woodworkers: I used a brush to lay on varnish, and the results were less than spectacular. Eventually I discovered wipe-on finishes, which produced a more attractive result. Still, I found the process slow and the available finishes limited. So I decided early on to learn how to spray finish. Because I had some experience with painting cars, I was somewhat familiar with

the process, and I knew how good the results could be.

Numerous compressors and spray guns later, I can say that I am fairly competent at spraying finishes. Although the road to proficiency was paved with drips and runs, spray finishing wasn't any more difficult than a lot of other woodworking techniques I've mastered. And unlike many woodworkers who still struggle with rags and brushes, I can honestly say that I enjoy

finishing. The tools are fun to use and I love the results.

Many woodworkers shy away from spraying finishes, wary of the need for more equipment, ventilation, overspray, dust problems, learning curve, etc. But the truth is, you can get by with just a few basic tools—a midsize compressor, a gravity-feed HVLP gun, and a cheap window fan—as long as you stick with water-based finishes. Let me repeat that: as long as you stick with water-based finishes. Solvent-based finishes, because of their flammability, must be sprayed with proper explosion-proof light fixtures and exhaust fan motors. The only exception is if you work outdoors away from any source of ignition.

—Anatole Burkin, editor-in-chief of *Fine Woodworking*

Think Finish First

BY JEFF JEWITT

BEFORE YOU START on your next furniture project, consider a finish's appearance, its method of application, and its durability.

Finishing is one of the biggest bugaboos for many woodworkers. Though they remain undaunted by complex joinery or intricate and precise machining, scores of woodworkers still cringe at the thought of applying a finish to their work. "What's the best finish for my project?" is a question I often hear. Being able to answer that question confidently and comfortably is an important hurdle to overcome.

Finishing products can be grouped into manageable categories, based on general working qualities and the degrees of protection they offer: waxes, oils, varnishes, shellacs, lacquers, and water-based finishes. Different finishes offer varying degrees of protection, durability, ease of application, repairability, and aesthetics. Unfortunately, no single finish excels in all categories—a finish that excels in one may fail in another—so in choosing a finish you must accept trade-offs.

As a professional refinisher, I routinely ask my customers a series of questions to determine the best finish for their furniture. I've modified my standard questions for this article and added a few as a checklist (facing page) for woodworkers trying to decide which finish to use on their own projects. Answers to these questions will point you toward the right finish to use on a given project, based on how well you need to protect the surface, how well the finish will hold up, how easy it is to apply, and how you want it to look. To get a better understanding of the choices, let's first take a look at the different categories of wood finishes.

An Overview of What's Out There

All wood finishes can be classified as one of two distinctly different types, based on how they dry, or cure. Evaporative finishes—such as lacquer, shellac, and many water-based finishes—dry to a hard film as the solvents evaporate. (Water is not a solvent—it's a carrier for the finish emulsion.) These types of finishes will always redissolve in the solvent used to thin them, long after they've dried, so they tend to be less durable than reactive finishes. Most reactive finishes—such as linseed or tung oil, catalyzed lacquers, and varnishes—also contain solvents that evaporate, but they cure by reacting with either air outside the can or a chemical placed in the can before application. These finishes undergo a chemical change as they cure, and after that they will not

To Determine the Best Finish, Ask the Right Questions

- How will the item be used? Will it be subjected to a lot of moisture, solvents, food, scrapes, and dents?
- What is your skill level, and how big is your work area? Does it stay clean, and is it heated and dry?
- What do you want the wood to look like? Do you want an "in-the-wood" natural look or a thicker film finish that accentuates depth?
- Will you be filling the pores to attain a highly polished finish?
- Will you be rubbing out the finish to achieve a particular sheen?
- Do you want the finish to alter the color of the wood? Is yellowing an issue? Do you want to minimize color changes as the wood ages?
- Safety and health: Are you sensitive to some solvents or concerned about flammability or the environmental impact of certain finishes?
- Toxicity of the finish: Will it be used near areas of food preparation?

APPEARANCE

1

APPLICATION

2

DURABLITY

3

redissolve in the solvent originally used to thin them. Except for the pure oils, reactive finishes tend to hold up better to heat and chemicals.

Waxes I don't consider wax an appropriate finish in and of itself. I use paste wax (carnauba mostly, sometimes beeswax) to polish furniture but only over other finishes, such as lacquer or shellac.

The True Oils Linseed oil and tung oil, the drying oils most often used in finishing, are readily available and relatively inexpensive. These finishes are called true oils to distinguish them from other products hyped as oil finishes and to separate them from naturally nondrying or semidrying oils used in finishes, such as soybean oil. These true oils change from a liquid to a solid through polymerization, a process that strengthens the cured finish.

Linseed oil is available in several forms. Unrefined, it's called raw linseed oil, which is rarely used on wood because it dries so slowly. Finishers long ago discovered that by boiling the oil, the resulting product was thicker and dried more quickly. Even though linseed oil that has actually been boiled is still available—it's called heat-treated or polymerized oil—most of the boiled linseed oil sold these days is raw oil that has been mixed with chemical additives to speed up the drying time. For wood finishing, you should use only boiled linseed oil.

Tung oil is derived from the nuts of trees that are native to Asia but have been cultivated in other parts of the world. Tung

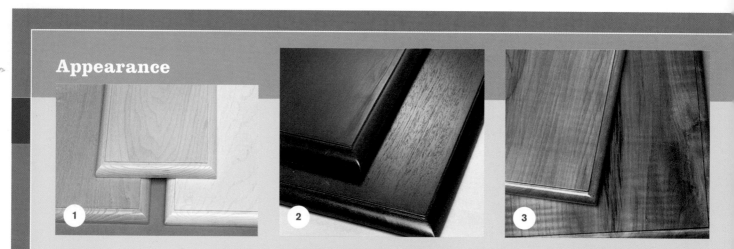

Appearance

1. On light-colored woods, the color of the finish matters. On these samples of ash, the warm, amber tone of nitrocellulose lacquer is just right. The orange shellac and water-based lacquer impart too much or too little color to the wood.

2. Do you want that tabletop filled? With the open pores of some woods (such as mahogany and walnut), and on large horizontal surfaces (such as dining tables), filled grain will make a huge difference in the way a finish looks.

3. The kind of finish you choose will greatly affect the way it looks. Some people prefer the flat look of oil finishes; others prefer a film finish such as the acrylic lacquer that reflects more light.

4. Most finishes turn yellow over time; some don't. To illustrate the difference, the author applied a CAB acrylic lacquer and a standard nitrocellulose lacquer over panels coated with white paint. The CAB acrylic lacquer is your best choice to avoid the effects of a yellowing finish.

5. Slow-drying finishes collect dust. Shellac and most lacquers dry so fast that small amounts of airborne dust don't pose a threat to the end result. Oil-based varnishes, on the

oil is available in a pure, unrefined form and in a heat-treated or polymerized form. The heat-treating process makes the oil a bit more durable and speeds up the drying time. It also minimizes a tendency of tung oil to "frost" (dry to a whitish, matte appearance). Tung oil is paler in color and has better moisture resistance than linseed oil.

Both linseed and tung oils are penetrating finishes, which means they penetrate the fibers of the wood and harden. These are the easiest finishes to apply: Wipe them on, allow them to penetrate the surface of the wood and wipe off the excess with a rag. These oils are usually not built up with enough coats to form a surface film, like that of varnish or lacquer, because the film is too soft.

Varnishes Varnish is made of tough and durable synthetic resins that have been modified with drying oils. Labels on cans of varnish will list resins such as alkyd, phenolic, and urethane, and the oils used are tung and linseed, as well as other semidrying oils such as soybean and safflower. Varnish cures by the same process as true oils—polymerization—but the resins make this finish more durable than oil. In fact, oil-based varnish is the most durable finish that can be easily applied by the average woodworker. Varnish surpasses most other finishes in its resistance to water, heat, solvents, and other chemicals.

Varnishes that contain a high percentage of oil are called long-oil varnishes. These include marine, spar, or exterior varnishes, and some interior varnishes for sale on the retail market. Long-oil varnishes are more

other hand, are virtual dust magnets and can be problematic in dusty shop environments.

6. Use oil as a sealer to highlight depth. The swipe of linseed oil across this curly maple tabletop shows what a difference it makes in bringing out the figure in the wood. You can apply a top coat of just about any other finish over a dried coat of oil.

7. A thinned finish goes on easier and looks better. Both of these samples of white oak have two coats of polyurethane varnish. The bottom sample was thinned to avoid the obvious buildup you can see on the top sample.

elastic and softer than medium- and short-oil varnishes that contain a lower percentage of oil. Medium-oil varnishes comprise most interior varnishes on the market. Short-oil varnishes (also known as heat-set varnishes and baking enamels) require extremely high temperatures to dry, so they're used only in industrial applications.

The type of resin used in the varnish determines the characteristics of the finish. Alkyd varnish is the standard all-purpose interior variety with decent protective qualities. Phenolic varnish, usually made with tung oil, is predominantly for exterior use. Urethane varnish, also called polyurethane, offers a better resistance to heat, solvents, and abrasions than any other varnish.

Varnish is typically applied with a brush, although a highly thinned and gelled version, called wiping varnish, can be applied with a rag.

Oil and varnish blends These mixtures, mostly oil with some varnish added, offer some of the best attributes of both ingredients: the easy application of true oils and the protective qualities of varnish. (Watco® Danish oil, teak oil, and a number of other finishes fall into this category.) It's difficult to ascribe accurate protective qualities to these products because manufacturers don't usually disclose the ratio of oil to varnish. Oil and varnish blends will dry a bit harder than true oils, and the finishes will build quicker with fewer applications.

Shellacs While most people think of shellac as a liquid finish found at a paint store, in its pure form it's a natural resin secreted from a bug that feeds on trees, mostly in India and Thailand. The secretions, in the form of cocoons, are gathered and eventually refined into dry flakes, which are then dissolved in denatured (ethyl) alcohol to make the shellac solution that winds up in cans at the store.

Shellac is available in several varieties. You can buy it premixed, or you can buy it in flake form and mix it yourself with denatured alcohol. The premixed variety is available in orange (amber) and clear, which is shellac that's been bleached. With the flakes, shellac is available in a wider variety of colors and wax contents than with the premixed version (which contains wax). The wax in shellac decreases the finish's resistance to water and prevents some finishes from bonding to it.

Lacquers Most professionals still regard lacquer as the best all-around finish for wood because it dries fast, imparts an incredible depth and richness to the wood, exhibits moderate to excellent durability (depending on the type used), and rubs out well. There are several different types of lacquer, and they exhibit different performance characteristics.

Nitrocellulose lacquer is the most common. If the label on the can says lacquer, it's most likely nitrocellulose, which is made from an alkyd and nitrocellulose resin dissolved and then mixed with solvents that evaporate quickly. This type of lacquer has moderate water resistance, but it's sensitive to heat and certain solvents. The biggest drawback is the finish's tendency to yellow as it ages, which shows clearly on light-colored woods.

Acrylic-modified lacquer is made from a mixture of a nonyellowing cellulose resin (called cellulose acetate butyrate, or CAB) and acrylic. This lacquer possesses the same general properties of nitrocellulose lacquer, except it is absolutely water-white, meaning it will not show as an amber color when applied over light-colored woods. Also, the finish won't turn yellow over time.

Catalyzed lacquer bridges the gap between the application traits of nitrocellulose lacquer and the durability of varnish. Catalyzed lacquer is a complex finish composed of urea formaldehyde or urea

A COMPARISON OF COMMON FINISH PRODUCTS

	Product	Ease of application	Repairability	Flame resistance	Health and safety	Water resistance	Chemical resistance	Scratch resistance
Evaporative finishes dry as their solvents disperse into the air. They will always redissolve into the solvent originally used to thin them, making them easier to repair but also a little less durable.	**Shellac**	Excellent	Excellent	Good	Good	Poor	Fair	Poor
	Nitro-cellulose lacquer	Good	Excellent	Fair	Excellent	Fair	Poor	Fair
	Most water-based finishes	Good	Poor	Excellent	Fair	Good	Good	Good
Reactive finishes undergo a chemical change as they cure, making them not only more difficult to repair but also more durable (except for linseed and tung oil) than most evaporative finishes.	**Linseed oil**	Excellent	Excellent	Good	Excellent	Poor	Fair	Poor
	Tung oil	Excellent	Excellent	Good	Excellent	Poor	Fair	Poor
	Oil-based varnish (alkyd resins)	Good	Poor	Good	Poor	Excellent	Good	Good
	Oil-based polyurethane	Good	Poor	Good	Poor	Excellent	Excellent	Excellent
	Most water-based finishes	Poor	Poor	Poor	Poor	Excellent	Excellent	Excellent

melamine and an alkyd that has some nitro-cellulose resin added to make it handle like normal lacquer. The addition of an acid catalyst initiates a chemical reaction that forms a very tough, durable finish. Catalyzed lacquer comes in two versions: precatalyzed and postcatalyzed. Precatalyzed lacquer has the components premixed, either by the manufacturer or at the store when you buy it; postcatalyzed lacquer is a two-part system that you must mix in your shop, following precise ratios. Once the catalyst has been added, these lacquers have a fairly short pot life (the time in which they can be used).

Water-Based Finishes Water-based finish contains some of the same ingredients as varnish and lacquer—notably urethane, alkyd, and acrylic—but many flammable and polluting ingredients have been replaced with water. The chemistry in this product is complex. Because the resins don't have a natural affinity for water, they must be chemically modified or forced to combine with water.

Water-based finish is usually made with either an acrylic resin (sold as water-based lacquer) or an acrylic urethane mixture (sold as water-based polyurethane). As with varnish, the addition of the urethane makes the resin tougher and more scratch resistant, but water-based urethane does not have the same solvent and heat resistance as its oil-based counterpart.

What Finishes Are More Durable?

The durability of a finish is measured by its resistance to water, chemicals, solvents (such as those in alkaline cleaners and acidic foods), heat, and scratches. Wax, shellac, lacquer, and some water-based finishes will be damaged if exposed to water long enough. Most of these products also scratch easily; however, they rub out well. (That's the flip side of scratch resistance.) Wax is surprisingly resistant to acids and alkalis. Aside from that, it is the least durable finish. Shellac is resistant neither to alkalis such as ammonia nor to alcohol. Of all the evaporative finishes, lacquer (nitrocellulose and acrylic, water-, and solvent-based) fares the best in terms of overall durability. Oil-based polyurethane is the most durable finish you can apply by hand, and catalyzed lacquer and varnish are the most durable sprayed finishes.

Choose a Finish to Match Your Skill Level

Your level of experience, the environment in which you work, and whether you're set up to spray all play a part in deciding which finish to use. The temperature and dampness of your shop, as well as the amount of

sanding dust in the air, will affect your choice. Dust falling onto a finish does not pose as great a problem with lacquer or shellac as it would with a slow-drying finish such as varnish. Shellac and lacquer are also the least temperamental when it comes to cold temperatures, and they can be modified with retarder additives for hot and humid conditions. Oils and oil-based products dry slowly in cold temperatures and humid conditions, and dust is always a problem when it has time to become embedded in the dried film.

Spray equipment requires a larger budget and, in most cases, expensive equipment to exhaust the overspray. There's also a learning curve with spraying, so it will likely take some practice before you get decent results.

The Type of Finish Will Notably Affect the Look of the Wood

Do you want a natural "in-the-wood" finish? Or does your work demand an elegant, deep, glass-smooth finish? Is the color of the finish a problem, or will yellowing of the finish be a problem down the road?

Traditionally, woodworkers have turned to oil, wax, or oil and varnish blends (such as Watco) for a natural-looking finish. None of these easy-to-apply finishes dries to form a hard surface film. However, you can get a natural-looking effect with any finish—including varnish, shellac, and lacquer—as long as you don't build it up more than a few coats and you rub out the dried film with steel wool. But if your goal is a filled-pore, deep, lustrous finish, you must use a hard, film-forming finish (varnish, shellac, or lacquer). This type of finish is also mandatory when you have to perform complex coloring options like toning and glazing.

Application

1. By atomizing the finish into a fine spray, you can achieve a smoother, more even finish faster than you can with any other method. You can spray shellac and oil-based varnishes (including polyurethane), as well as water-based, nitrocellulose, and catalyzed lacquers.

2. Whether you use a disposable sponge brush or the more traditional bristles, laying on a coat of finish with a brush will require fewer applications. Careful technique means everything toward the goal of a neat job. Brushes work best with oil- and water-based varnishes.

3. The time-honored French polish is essentially many coats of shellac put on with a rag. You can apply oils as well as varnishes using this method, which is time-consuming but almost foolproof. Wiping on a finish requires patience.

The color and the penetration of the finish itself may be an issue. Orange shellac and phenolic-resin varnish both have colors that may be too dark for woods that you may want to keep as light as possible. In addition, many finishes deepen or darken the wood surface. In most cases this is desirable, because it adds depth and increases luster. However, you may want to downplay any deepening effect. Some delicately figured woods (such as pearwood) will appear muddy when an oil finish is applied.

Oil and oil-based varnish, solvent-based lacquer, and shellac all deepen the color of the wood and increase surface luster the most. These finishes wet the cells of the wood, penetrating into the surface. Other film finishes—notably water-based finishes and some catalyzed lacquers—tend to lie on the surface. By not penetrating it as much, they make the wood appear lighter in color.

The plastic look that's sometimes ascribed to polyurethane and catalyzed lacquers has more to do with the incorrect application of these finishes than it does with the finishes themselves. On open-pored woods (plainsawn ash or oak, for example) the application of thick varnish and lacquer can result in a soupy look on the surface. This is a consequence of the finish film bridging across the open pores rather than flowing into them. By thinning these finishes, you can achieve more attractive results. My favorite method to apply oil-based polyurethane is to thin the finish 50 percent with mineral spirits and wipe it on.

A finish film that turns yellow with age will be noticeable with unstained, light-colored woods such as maple or birch. An acrylic finish, water- or solvent-based, does not have this problem. Paste wax and some catalyzed finishes also will not yellow.

Think About Safety and the Environment

A solvent-based finish, such as varnish and lacquer, contains a good deal of organic solvents, which can affect the environment as well as your health. It's also highly flammable. If these particulars pose a problem for you, use a water-based finish to eliminate the fire hazard and to mitigate the environmental and health impact. Pure oil is a surprisingly good alternative to a solvent-based lacquer or varnish: Pure oil contains no solvents and comes from renewable resources. However, oil-soaked rags must be disposed of carefully. Shellac

Durability

1. Catalyzed lacquers and conversion varnishes will hold up to heat damage better than any other finishes.
2. Alcohol is the original solvent for shellac, an evaporative finish, and will melt right into the dried film in no time.
3. Standing water (from a leaky vase or one that collected condensed moisture from the air) can wreak havoc on most finishes. Catalyzed lacquers and oil-based varnishes fare the best against moisture damage.
4. A dining table might make a nice racetrack—especially to a child who hasn't noticed his rubber tires are missing. Polyurethane and catalyzed lacquers resist scratches better than any other finishes.
5. Damage to an evaporative finish, such as the shellac on the surface of this cherry table, is relatively easy to fix.

is also a good alternative. The solvent for shellac, denatured alcohol, is distilled from corn, and most people don't find the fleeting odor objectionable.

All finishes are nontoxic when fully cured, despite what you may have read or heard. Once the solvents have evaporated, any cured film is safe for contact with food. This does not mean that the finish itself is safe to gobble up. It means simply that additives such as heavy-metal driers and plasticizers are encapsulated well enough that they do not migrate into your food. Wax and shellac (apples and candy are coated with these) are the only edible finishes that I'm aware of, besides mineral oil, which is sold as a laxative.

Spraying wastes a great deal of the finish material, and the organic solvents are dispersed into the air. Brushing or wiping on a finish is a practical, though less speedy, alternative.

JEFF JEWITT restores furniture in Cleveland, Ohio, and is the author of *Taunton's Complete Illustrated Guide to Finishing* (2004).

Using Waterborne Finishes

BY ANDY CHARRON

Before I owned any spray equipment, I used brushes or rags to apply solvent-based finishes. When I finally purchased a spray gun, I had a limited amount of money and very little shop space, so I could not set up a proper spray booth. I sought out finishes that were non-flammable and relatively safe to use. Waterborne lacquers were the obvious choice. All I needed was a fan for air circulation and a clean place to spray.

It took trial and error, but now I get consistently even coats of finish that are smooth and free of defects. I've also discovered that I don't have to use spray equipment to get good results. A number of waterborne finishes can be successfully applied with brushes or pads. Even though I now have the shop equipment to spray solvent-based lacquers and varnishes, I use waterborne finishes 90 percent of the time.

Many states now regulate the amount of solvent or volatile organic compounds (VOCs) that may be released into the air by professional shops. This has led to the development of more user-friendly and less-toxic waterborne finishes. However, waterborne products are still very different from their solvent-based counterparts. If they are not applied properly, they can be frustrating to work with and can yield disappointing results. Knowing what problems to expect and understanding how to overcome them will help make waterborne finishes easier to apply.

Success depends on several factors: surface preparation; compatibility of sealers, stains, and topcoats; material preparation; application methods; and even the weather. My methods are applicable to waterborne urethanes, lacquers, enamels, dyes, sealers, and primers.

Prepare the Surface by Raising the Grain

If you have ever spilled water on a freshly sanded piece of wood, you may have noticed how the grain stands up, creating a rough surface. All waterborne finishes have this effect on wood. Earlier versions contained more water than the newer formulations, so grain-raising isn't as bad as it used to be. The resins used today are lighter and more viscous, and they require less water in their formulations. But no matter how much you sand bare wood, all waterborne finishes will raise the grain at least enough to require some additional sanding (see the top right photo on p. 16).

The simplest way to deal with raised grain is to surrender to it. First, finish-sand workpieces as you normally would with a

Surface Preparation

WATERBORNE FINISHES WILL RAISE THE GRAIN. Apply a sanding sealer over a stain or dye before any top coats. Sanding sealers contain lubricants, which make them easy to sand.

WATERBORNE DYES ARE RUBBED ON WITH A RAG. Flood the workpiece when applying stains and dyes. Work quickly, and wipe off any excess to avoid lap marks.

DON'T USE TACK RAGS TO WIPE OFF DUST. They can leave chemical residues that will show up as blemishes under a waterborne finish. Use a rag dampened with water.

sandpaper in the 180-grit to 220-grit range, and then intentionally raise the grain. You can use water, sanding sealer, or dewaxed shellac. If you use water, lightly dampen a sponge or a rag, and wipe the workpiece. Or you can dampen the wood with a plant mister. Let the workpiece dry to the touch, and then sand with 220-grit to 400-grit paper. A waterborne finish, when applied over this surface, will not raise the grain very much. A light sanding after the first coat is required, but you would be performing this step when using a solvent-based finish, too.

I usually raise the grain with a coat of sanding sealer instead of water. Most manufacturers offer sealers that are designed for their products. Sealers are usually formulated with stearates, which act as lubricants and make sanding easier. If you can't find a sealer, shellac works very well.

If the wood needs to be colored, I use one coat of water-soluble dye to raise the grain and then follow with a coat of sealer or shellac. When that dries, sand it. The sealer or shellac stiffens the fibers raised by the dye, making them much easier to sand. The sealer also gives you a buffer that keeps you from sanding through the dye to bare wood so quickly.

The amount of grain raised will vary with the type of wood. Open-grained woods, such as oak, will require more sanding than closed-grain woods, such as maple. I use wet-or-dry sandpaper in the 220-grit to 400-grit range, depending on how fine a surface I'm after. I don't use sandpapers that contain stearates. Small stearate particles that aren't cleaned off the workpiece surface will cause surface defects called fisheyes when waterborne finishes are applied over them. After sanding, use a slightly damp, lint-free cloth to wipe off the dust (see the bottom right photo on the facing page). By the time you get out your brushes or set up your spray equipment, the workpiece will be dry enough for a finish. Do not use tack rags because the resins in them can react with the finish and leave blemishes.

Make Sure All Finishing Products Are Compatible

Waterborne top coats must be compatible with any other fillers, stains, or dyes that are applied. Most waterborne materials have improved, and many are now compatible with solvent-based products. That does not mean that all materials will be compatible in all cases.

If, for example, you plan to apply waterborne lacquer over pigmented oil stain, give the oil-based product enough time to cure fully. Before applying the waterborne product, rough up the surface with a very fine-grit sandpaper so the first coat has a better chance to bite into the stain. Sometimes, two products demonstrate their incompatibility immediately, and the top coat will bead up or not flow out. Problems such as blistering can manifest themselves several days later. If you're unsure about compatibility, experiment on a piece of scrap.

The best way to eliminate any doubt about the compatibility of two products is to apply a barrier coat of sealer between them. The best sealer I have found is dewaxed shellac. Although you can buy shellac that has the wax already removed, often referred to as blond shellac, it can be hard to find and usually comes in large quantities. I buy clear, premixed shellac in a 3-lb. cut and keep it undisturbed for a day or two until the wax settles to the bottom of the can. Then I pour off the clear top fluid. I thin it down to 2:1 with denatured alcohol. Then I apply a fairly heavy, even coat of this, let it dry for about a half hour and lightly sand with 220-grit (or finer)

paper. The shellac not only seals in the first coat but helps the two potentially incompatible materials bond. It's never failed for me.

Thoroughly Mix and Strain Finishing Materials

Most waterborne finishes are designed to be used straight from the can and do not require thinning. The only thing you need to do before applying them is to stir up the solids that settle to the bottom of the can. These solids have a tendency to separate or settle out over time and may require a lot of stirring to get back into solution. The older the material, the more likely it contains lumps. As a final precaution, I always strain it through a plastic, paper, or nylon-mesh filter.

Occasionally, you may need to thin a finish such as a thick, pigmented primer because it doesn't flow or spray well. Unlike

traditional nitrocellulose lacquers, which can be thinned almost indefinitely, waterborne finishes are extremely sensitive and don't respond well to thinning. Waterborne materials contain carefully measured amounts of various chemicals, including solvents, water, defoaming agents, and resins. Adding another material to the mix can upset this balance. When that happens, the finish may be prone to runs and drips because it takes too long to dry.

If the finish isn't flowing out properly after brushing, check with the manufacturer to see if a flow additive is available. As a last resort, try adding small amounts (3 percent to 5 percent by volume) of clean water. Ideally, you should use distilled water, but I have used plain tap water without any noticeable ill effects. If the finish seems to go on too dry when spraying in hot, dry conditions, you might want to add a retarder (the surface will look and feel fuzzy).

Choosing an Application Method

There are differences between waterborne top coats made for spraying and those meant for brushing or padding. A spray finish is just that. If you try brushing it, the material may foam or dry too quickly. But I've found that any finish made for brushing can be sprayed with good results.

Most waterborne stains and dyes don't require any special application equipment and can be wiped or sprayed just like solvent-based stains. However, because waterborne products dry so quickly (in particular, water-soluble dyes), you will have to move rapidly when wiping them on. Be sure to flood the surface with a full, wet coat to avoid lap marks.

I usually get a good finish with two applications of top coat. For added durability, such as you might need on a tabletop, I'd recommend three or more coats. Although waterborne finishes don't release the kind of noxious fumes some solvent-based finishes do, they still give off some vapors. So I take precautions. If I'm brushing finishes, I make do with some cross ventilation. When I'm spraying, I wear a respirator with organic vapor filters and ventilate the work area.

Select a synthetic bristle brush for finishing Natural bristles will absorb the water in waterborne products and begin to splay and lose their shape. Synthetic bristles won't. When applying a finish, keep the brush wet, and don't scrape the bristles against the edge of the can (see the top left photo). Let the excess material drip back into the container. This takes a little longer, but it will help prevent foaming. Then apply the material on the workpiece in a thin coat. Put it on too thick, and you will get runs and sags. Always work quickly and from a wet edge to avoid lap marks.

The more you brush the finish, the greater the likelihood it will begin to foam

Brushing the Finish

LET THE EXCESS FINISH DRIP OFF THE BRUSH. Rubbing the brush against the edge of the container may cause the finish to foam.

OTHER CAUSES OF FOAMING: If you shake a can of waterborne finish instead of stirring it, you'll have a problem with bubbles.

ONCE YOU'VE STARTED, work from a wet surface to a dry section. Brush quickly and with the grain; let the bristles skate off the workpiece surface to lessen brush marks.

Spraying the Finish

BEGIN SPRAYING BEFORE YOU REACH THE WORKPIECE. Hold the gun 4 in. to 6 in. away from the workpiece, and spray at a speed that makes the surface wet and shiny but not runny.

MANY WATERBORNE FINISHES look milky white when first applied. The section closest to the author already shows signs of clearing up as he works toward the center of the table.

DON'T STOP BEFORE THE EDGE. Keep spraying until the pattern falls off the edge of the work-piece. On the next pass, overlap the previous section.

and bubble. If you experience foaming, add a flow additive for the finish, if one is available. If not, as a last resort, try adding a few drops of lacquer thinner, mineral spirits, or milk to the finish. These additives can reduce the surface tension of the finish and improve flow. Disposable foam or sponge brushes and paint pads also work with waterborne materials. Apply the finish over the surface using quick, light passes.

Spraying gives the best results A spray gun allows you to apply a full, even coat over an entire piece in a manner of minutes. The finish dries so quickly that, in most cases, you will be able to apply several coats in one day.

Because waterborne finishes contain a higher percentage of solids than most other finishes, they have a tendency to run or sag if applied too heavily. When spraying, lay on just enough material to leave a shiny, wet sheen on the surface of the wood, but not so wet that it begins to run.

If you catch a run or drip while it is still wet, wipe it off with a clean, lint-free cloth, and recoat the area immediately. Otherwise, use a razor blade to cut off any dried or skinned-over trouble spots, sand, and recoat.

Spray equipment that's made of plastic or stainless steel is best for use with waterborne products because those materials won't rust. But if your gun is made of metals that can corrode, you can ward off rust by drying it thoroughly after use by blowing compressed air through it. You can also remove any residual water by running a few ounces of denatured alcohol through the gun.

Weather Conditions Affect Finishes

The cooperation of Mother Nature can certainly make a difference when applying finishes. When waterborne materials are applied on dry, warm days, they flow out smoothly, level quickly, and dry to the touch in less than an hour, sometimes in a matter of minutes when spraying. Under ideal conditions (around 70°F with 35 percent to 50 percent relative humidity), you can apply several coats in one day. However, if your finishing room is cold or the humidity is high, waterborne products can become downright ornery.

When waterborne products are cold, they don't atomize properly, don't flow out well, and take longer than normal to dry. Ideally, you should heat your finishing room. But there's another way. I've found that if I heat the finish to about 75° right before using it, I can apply top coats in a room as cold as 45°F. All I do is place the can of finish in a sink or bucket full of hot water for a few minutes. (Never use a stove or open flame to heat any kind of finish material.) Warm finish is easy to spray, flows out well, and dries quickly.

Lowering the humidity can be more difficult. In a small room, a dehumidifier can reduce the moisture content. But I have a large shop near the ocean and no equipment to reduce humidity. I have found that a fan blowing warm air over the piece being finished can offset the negative effects of high humidity.

Waterborne finishes, like other top coats, can be rubbed out to increase or decrease their sheen. Just remember to avoid steel wool, which can cause black spots if pieces of it lodge in the finish and rust.

ANDY CHARRON operates Charron Wood Products in Windsor, Vermont.

New Water-Based Finishes

BY ANDY CHARRON

A lot of woodworkers won't get near water-based finishes because they believe these products cause excessive grain raising, don't adhere well over oil-based stains, and look like plastic. When I first began using water-based finishes about eight years ago, these products were indeed difficult to use and didn't look so hot. That's not the case anymore. Water-based finishes are getting better all the time. Also, they don't give off noxious fumes, they dry fast, and they aren't flammable.

TARGET® ENTERPRISES OXFORD HYBRID GLOSS VARNISH
Good depth, warm tone. Closely approaches lacquer in appearance. Doesn't do well over oil-based stain.

PARKS PRO FINISHER POLYURETHANE
Only a very slight blue tint (approaching neutral) and good depth. Fills pores well.

J.E. MOSER® COOL-LAC
The first water-based shellac. Has a warm color, but finish is very thin and doesn't build well, which makes it difficult to rub out without cutting through coats.

SHERWIN-WILLIAMS® KEM AQUA
Commercial spray finish, available only in 5-gal. containers. Slightly blue tint and cloudy. More difficult than average to apply.

COMPLIANT SPRAY SYSTEMS ENDURO WAT-R-BASE® POLY OVERPRINT
Top-rated finish with a warm tone and good depth. Closely approaches lacquer in appearance.

HYDROCOTE® RESISTHANE PRE-CATALYZED LACQUER
Slightly blue tint, cloudy. Easy to apply.

FSM CORP. CLEARLY SUPERIOR 455
Slightly blue tint, cloudy. Fills pores well but difficult to rub to an even gloss.

VAN TECHNOLOGIES VANAQUA URETHANE
Neutral tone but slightly cloudy. Builds and fills pores quickly.

A survey in *Fine Woodworking* magazine evaluated 15 water-based finishes. Manufacturers have been busy, and there's a whole new crop of finishes on the market. I tried nine new finishes and compared them with a couple of time-tested finishes: nitrocellulose lacquer and shellac. I also compared the new finishes to Famowood® Super Lac, a water-based finish that did extremely well in the previous evaluation, especially when measured on appearance.

The new finishes really stand out when it comes to stain resistance. Most were bulletproof. Grain raising wasn't objectionable with the majority of the finishes, and a few barely raised the grain at all. Some of the finishes were difficult to apply, although most went on without a hitch.

Rating the products on appearance is the most subjective test, but an important one, and several finishes scored very high. Even the finishes that scored low on appearance are light-years ahead of what I was using five years ago. It's fair to say that water-based finishes are getting better, and I imagine the trend will continue.

Resins and Additives Have Been Improved

Traditional finishes such as lacquer and shellac have very few ingredients, primarily resins (solids that form the finish film) and

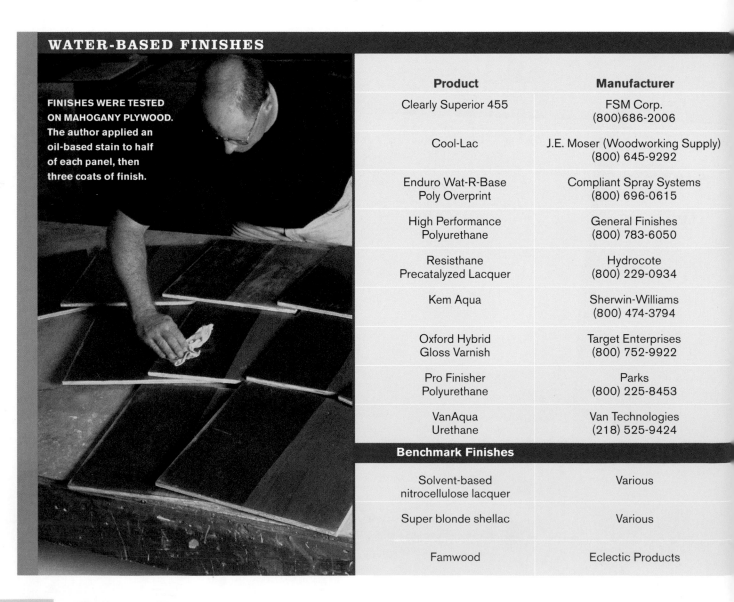

WATER-BASED FINISHES

FINISHES WERE TESTED ON MAHOGANY PLYWOOD. The author applied an oil-based stain to half of each panel, then three coats of finish.

Product	Manufacturer
Clearly Superior 455	FSM Corp. (800)686-2006
Cool-Lac	J.E. Moser (Woodworking Supply) (800) 645-9292
Enduro Wat-R-Base Poly Overprint	Compliant Spray Systems (800) 696-0615
High Performance Polyurethane	General Finishes (800) 783-6050
Resisthane Precatalyzed Lacquer	Hydrocote (800) 229-0934
Kem Aqua	Sherwin-Williams (800) 474-3794
Oxford Hybrid Gloss Varnish	Target Enterprises (800) 752-9922
Pro Finisher Polyurethane	Parks (800) 225-8453
VanAqua Urethane	Van Technologies (218) 525-9424
Benchmark Finishes	
Solvent-based nitrocellulose lacquer	Various
Super blonde shellac	Various
Famwood	Eclectic Products

solvents (also called carriers), which dissolve the resins. Water-based finishes are similar in that they, too, contain resins and solvents. But water-based finishes have many more additives than traditional lacquers, sometimes as many as 20, to deal with the basic incompatibility of water and resin. The other chemicals, especially ones called surfactants, allow water and resins to mix together, forming an emulsion. As the water evaporates, alcohols or cosolvents soften the resins, allowing them to coalesce and form the finish film.

Although manufacturers are unwilling to give away trade secrets, they did tell me they've made headway with the types of resins and additives used in finishes. These improvements translate to finishes that bond better to solvent-based products and are tougher, yet easier to sand and rub out.

With the exception of one water-based shellac, the resins in the water-based finishes I tested are acrylic, urethane, or a combination of both. These finishes go by many descriptive terms, including lacquer, polyurethane, or varnish, but for purposes of discussion, most water-based finishes are technically lacquers, meaning they can be redissolved by their own solvents.

Adhesion over oil-based stain	Stain resistance (22 max)	Heat resistance	Raised grain	Sanding	Best applicator	Appearance
Pass	19	Fail	Moderate to heavy	Moderate	Brush or spray	Poor
Pass	22	Fail	Moderate	Easy	Brush	Good
Pass	21	Pass	Minor	Easy	Spray	Excellent
Pass	20	Pass	Minor	Easy	Brush or spray	Good
Pass	20	Pass	Heavy	Moderate	Brush or spray	Fair
Pass	22	Fail	Moderate	Moderate	Spray	Fair
Fail	22	Pass	Moderate	Moderate	Brush or spray	Excellent
Pass	22	Pass	Moderate	Moderate	Brush or spray	Good
Pass	22	Fail	Moderate	Moderate	Spray	Good
Pass	21	Pass	Minor	Easy	Spray	Excellent
Pass	16	Fail	Moderate	Easy	Brush or spray	Good
Pass	22	Pass	Moderate	Easy	Spray	Excellent

Finishes Were All Tested the Same Way

I used squares cut from the same sheet of mahogany plywood to test all the finishes (see the photo on p. 24). First, I applied a coat of Minwax® red-mahogany oil-based stain to half of each panel. I allowed the stain to dry for two days, then applied three coats of finish to each panel, using either a brush, a spray gun, or a combination of both, going by manufacturers' recommendations. I let each coat dry for a minimum of two hours before lightly sanding and applying another coat. Although some manufacturers offer sanding sealers, all of the products I tested can be used on bare wood, and that's what I did. Then I subjected the panels to common household chemicals to see how they would hold up.

After I had finished with the various tests, I sanded the top coats using 240-grit, 400-grit, and 600-grit sandpaper, then rubbed them with pumice and rottenstone. I also tested traditional shellac, nitrocellulose lacquer, and a previously tested water-based product for comparison.

Testing adhesion over an oil-based stain The adhesion test determines if a water-based finish will stick to an oil-based stain. I used a sharp knife or razor to slice an X into the finish where it was applied over the stain. Then I placed a piece of packing tape over the X and pressed down firmly. I let the tape sit for about 5 minutes and then yanked it off (see the photo above). The finish held fast on eight panels. Only one finish chipped off, failing the test.

Common foods were used for the stain test I gave each finish what I call the kitchen-table test. Tables are subjected to food spills, and a good finish should survive the onslaught as well as the chemicals used to clean up the mess.

I placed a small amount of the following common household products on each panel: milk, orange juice, hot coffee, mustard, ketchup, red wine, grape jelly, vinegar, olive oil, Windex®, and Fantastik® (see the top photo on the facing page). After one hour, I wiped each spot off, checking for damage. If there was no damage, the finish received 2 points. If the finish was slightly damaged (dull), it got 1 point. If the finish was severely stained, damaged or eaten away, it got no points. All of the finishes I tested scored at least 19 points, and several got a perfect 22. Windex and Fantastik caused the most damage.

FOOD-STAIN TEST. **Finishes were subjected to a variety of common foods and cleaners. Most finishes held up very well. Cleaning products, however, were hardest on the finishes.**

A finish for a table needs to withstand heat Tables are often exposed to hot pots, cups, and spoons. To re-create this scenario, I put a spoon in boiling water for a few minutes, then placed it on a test panel. After the spoon had cooled, I removed it. If the spoon left no mark, the finish passed the test. If the spoon stuck to the finish or left a dull impression, it failed.

New products are easier to sand and rub out Water-based finishes have a reputation for causing excessive grain raising and for being difficult to sand. A simple way to gauge the roughness is to brush a finger across the first coat after it dries.

The first coat of finish causes most, if not all, the grain raising. In my test, if a panel felt rough, like medium-grit sandpaper, I rated the raised grain as "heavy." If the panel felt more like fine sandpaper, I rated it "moderate." If it felt like very fine sandpaper, I rated it "minor."

To determine whether a finish was easy or difficult to sand, I sanded all three coats

HOT-SPOON TEST. **Several finishes were marred when a hot spoon was allowed to cool on the panel.**

TOO-THIN FINISHES ARE TRICKY TO SAND. **Some finishes, such as J.E. Moser's Cool-Lac, a water-based shellac, go on so thin that it's difficult not to sand through to previous coats.**

with varying grits of fresh paper. I not only looked at how easily the finish powdered up and how much it clogged the paper, but I also considered how hard I had to work to achieve a smooth, flat surface. Thankfully, all of the finishes I tested fell in the easy to moderate range. In fact, several of the finishes were as easy or easier to sand than lacquer and shellac. For a high-gloss, rubbed-out finish, I found that using 1,000-grit and 1,200-grit wet abrasive paper (available at auto-body supply shops) prior to rubbing out with pumice and rottenstone gave me the best results.

Appearance is the most subjective test
Because most of the finishes scored well in the kitchen-table tests, the deciding factor comes down to looks. Admittedly, this is subjective. Something that looks good to me may not look good to you. To give a fair evaluation, I showed the panels to a couple of other professional woodworkers and weighed their opinions as well as my own. I used solvent-based lacquer as the benchmark against which all the finishes were judged for appearance. Lacquer imbues wood with a warm tone, what I call a light amber color, and the finish also has clarity, which adds depth, especially after three coats or more. The best of the finishes approached this look. I downgraded finishes if they had a slightly cool or blue cast and were dull or cloudy.

Overall, the New Products Tested Well

If the color of the finish were not an issue, I would consider using any one of these products, with the exception of J.E. Moser's Cool-Lac. Although the Cool-Lac scored well on the tests (better than traditional shellac) and had a true shellac color, I found it difficult to apply. The product is very thin, nearly the consistency of water, and contains a low level of solids. As a result, the coats go on very thin and don't build well. Building a deep, protective finish requires half a dozen coats or more.

My two favorite finishes are the Compliant Spray Systems Enduro Wat-R-Base Poly Overprint and Target Enterprises Oxford Hybrid Gloss Varnish. Enduro and Oxford look virtually identical to solvent-based lacquer. They give wood a warm tone and highlight the grain because of their clarity. Both are easy to apply, but the Enduro requires only three coats to develop a good build. When I went to rub out the Oxford after three coats, I cut through to bare wood before achieving a nice shine. You need to apply at least five coats if you plan to rub this finish out to a high gloss.

If I had to choose between the two, I would opt for the Enduro, because it dries incredibly fast and because it passed the adhesion test. I think most people would be hard-pressed to tell the difference between Enduro and solvent-based lacquer. The Oxford finish—which, like the Enduro, has a nice, warm tone—didn't adhere well over an oil-based stain (it held fine over bare wood). You can solve this problem by using a water- or alcohol-based stain or by applying a sealer of shellac between the oil stain and the finish. Not to be forgotten, Eclectic Products Famowood Super Lac, a finish that tested well in previous tests, ranks right up there with the Enduro and Oxford. It's easy to handle and apply. It rubs out extremely well, has good depth, and has a color very similar to that of nitrocellulose lacquer.

ANDY CHARRON operates Charron Wood Products in Windsor, Vermont.

Improving the Color of Water-Based Finishes

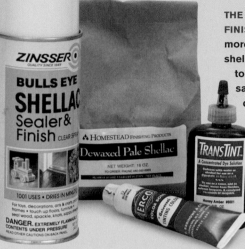

Although some water-based products have improved to the point where they appear comparable in color to traditional lacquer or shellac right out of the can, others still have a way to go. Some look a bit bland, and others suffer from a very slight bluish cast. If you happen to like everything about your finish except its color, consider toning the wood or the finish.

Some finish manufacturers tone their products for customers who prefer a warm look. The Enduro Wat-R-Base Poly Overprint has an additive that gives the finish a slight amber tone. Hydrocote offers an amber additive that can be added to its finishes. There are other products available to help you color top coats. Whatever you do, don't thin the finish beyond what the manufacturer recommends.

TINTING THE WOOD

Using shellac for a first, or sealer, coat will impart a warm glow to wood. It will also raise and stiffen the grain, making it easy to sand. Use fresh-mixed shellac that is dewaxed. You can also color the wood using dyes. A thin coat of a highly diluted water-soluble dye should give the wood just the right hint of color.

COLORING THE TOP COAT

In some cases, you may want to color the top coat itself. What you are actually doing is using the finish as a toner, which can be a bit tricky.

Pigments should be used in small amounts: You can use universal tinting colors (UTCs), which are available at paint stores, to alter the appearance of a clear finish. A small drop or two of an earthy tone like burnt umber or raw sienna goes a long way toward giving an otherwise bland finish a sense of color and warmth. However, pigments are opaque and may give the finish a dark, cloudy, or muddy appearance. If you use pigments to color a clear coat, use them sparingly and take great pains to apply the finish as evenly as possible.

THE COLOR OF SOME WATER-BASED FINISHES can be improved. To bring more warmth to a finish, dewaxed shellac can be applied as a sealer coat to bare wood. Or you can add universal tinting color (tube) or dissolved dye (bottle) directly to a finish to change its tone.

Water-soluble dyes are preferred: A better alternative to pigments are water-soluble dyes. Dissolve a small amount of dye in water first and then add a few drops at a time to the finish until the color is right. Remember, water will thin the finish, so use it sparingly. Because dyes are transparent, they won't give the finish a muddy look. Dyes, however, will not penetrate the resins; they really only color the liquid part of the finish, which will evaporate, leaving the dye in place. This can cause some blotching.

Alcohol dyes are the best way to tint finishes: Dyes that have been dissolved in alcohol will actually penetrate the resins in a finish and change their colors. The resulting finish is even in tone and uniform in color. I like to use TransTint® honey amber from Homestead Finishing Products (440-582-8929), which comes in concentrated liquid form. Add four to six drops per quart of finish as a starting point to impart a warm tone.—A.C.

ADD DYE SPARINGLY. A few drops of amber dye added to a neutral or slightly blue finish will give it a warm tone.

Tips for Better Sanding

BY
LON SCHLEINING

PICKING THE RIGHT SANDING TOOL

When I tell students in my wood-working classes at Cerritos College that sanding is one of my favorite activities, they usually look at me like I'm a little cracked. But the truth is, I look forward to sanding—especially that last hand-sanding, which tells me I've finished another job. With thoughtful planning and the right tools, sanding doesn't have to be tedious.

I approach sanding in two stages: shaping and smoothing. If the piece still needs some work after it is cut and pared with other tools, then sanding tools can complete the shaping. If I'm working on a curved piece with changing grain direction, for example, I can shape it more easily with a sanding tool than with an edge tool. There is also less chance of tearing out the grain.

FLATTENING A TABLETOP

FAIRING A CURVE

Shaping uses 80-grit to 120-grit sandpaper and powerful tools. I use a 4-in. by 24-in. belt sander, 5-in. and 8-in. rotary disc sanders, a right-angle random-orbit sander, an inflatable, handheld drum sander, and a spindle sander—whatever best fits the job I'm up against. During shaping, I sand until I can no longer spot any machine marks, lumps, glue marks, or deep scratches. If I find rough patches, I go back to shaping with 100-grit sandpaper before I begin smoothing.

Smoothing usually involves using less aggressive machines and paper grits of 120 and finer. I use an orbital sander, palm- and pistol-grip random-orbit sanders, as well as hand-sanding blocks of various shapes and sizes—both flexible and rigid. If this sounds like a lot of sanding tools, it is. It just boils down to the fact that it takes different tools to handle different jobs efficiently.

Both sanding stages are best done sooner rather than later—ideally, prior to assembly. This usually saves me from sanding for long periods of time, and it also keeps me from sanding into tight spots. A drawer is a good example. If the interior pieces of a drawer need sanding, do so before assem-

bling the drawer. This way the sanding can be done in minutes without the difficulty of sanding into inside corners. Any miters or frame-and-panel assemblies can be handled the same way, saving countless frustrations. Then after assembly, usually only a light hand-sanding is needed before the finish is applied.

Sanding involves removing all of the machine marks and the scratches left by rougher-grit sandpaper. Then, using finer and finer grits, the scratches from the previous sandpaper are reduced until the piece is smooth. Often, grains come off the paper as the sanding takes place. And if larger sanding grains from earlier grits are left on the surface, they can be rubbed into the board and gouge the wood. You can prevent this by vacuuming dust and sanding debris before moving to finer grits.

WHETHER FAIRING A CURVE or flattening a tabletop, the right tools and techniques yield quality results.

Tuning and Using a Belt Sander

On most projects, my belt sander is the first tool I reach for. I've heard countless horror stories from students and woodworkers about projects they've destroyed with belt sanders, but with a few adjustments and a little practice, it's an invaluable tool.

One big problem I've noticed is that the stock sheet-metal platens on most belt sanders are rarely flat from the beginning, much less after hours of use. As the belt rubs against and heats the platen, the metal distorts, creating a convex platen that will leave a dished-out sanding pattern. Luckily, platens are easily replaced with graphite-coated canvas (see the photo below), the material normally used on larger sanding tools. The canvas is available from Klingspor® (800-228-0000).

A belt sander must sit flat on the surface to do its job. Start with the sander resting on the work. When you pull the trigger, the machine will lurch forward a bit. But once it starts sanding, simply let it float on the surface. Keep it moving, but don't grip the handles so tightly that you tilt the machine or prevent it from floating across the surface.

A SANDING FRAME TAMES A BELT SANDER. A sanding frame rides on the surface, suspending the sander above the work. The amount of sanding pressure actually applied to the project is more easily controlled than when using the sander alone.

Practice helps. Cover a surface with pencil marks to see whether you're actually sanding where you think you are. Then sand only a few seconds between inspections. You might be surprised to see that you didn't sand where you thought you did, and vice versa. You'll see that to sand out to the edge, the sander must hang about half its length over the edge.

If you're as frustrated with a belt sander as some of my students are, try a sanding frame. A frame helps control a portable belt sander so that it sands evenly (see the photo above). Sanding frames are now available from most sander manufacturers, and though the investment is small, the difference is tremendous, especially if you're just starting out.

AN UNEVEN SANDER WON'T FLATTEN ANYTHING. The author replaces a belt sander's metal platen with graphite-coated canvas using the old platen as a pattern. A new, flat platen can make a big difference in a machine's performance.

The first step toward efficient sanding is to make sure you remove all of the scratches from the previous tool. I spend more time (80 percent) with the rougher grits and less time (20 percent) with the finer grits. If you sand thoroughly with each grit and move from one grit to the next without skipping, no single grit takes a long time. After removing milling marks with 100 grit, don't skip 120 and 150 grits. No matter how long you sand, 180-grit paper will not remove scratches made by 100-grit paper. And when you're sanding, sand the entire project one grit at a time. Sanding only part of the project will inevitably result in a poorly sanded project, and the finish will suffer.

Use finer-grit sandpaper on rougher, more aggressive tools. I rarely use grit even as rough as 80 on my belt, orbital, or disk sanders. One hundred grit is just about as fast and won't leave such deep scratches.

Remember that even though the grit itself is finer on 100-grit paper than it is on 80 grit, there is more of it—so the cutting speed is often the same. The harder the wood, the harder it is to remove scratches. On woods like hard maple, it is very difficult to remove the scratches left by using rougher grits like 80 or even 100. You can alleviate this problem by starting with 120-grit or finer paper.

Most woodworkers have heard the expression, "Let the tool do the work." No where is this more applicable than with sanding. The machine should supply the power. The sandpaper should supply the cutting action. All the operator should supply is guidance, not downward pressure. If you find that you're applying so much downward pressure that you're getting tired, chances are your sandpaper is too dull or your machine is too light for the job.

Using Orbital and Random-Orbit Machines

An orbital sander is a wonderful tool, but if used incorrectly, it can ruin a nice project in seconds. A tool long relied upon in the boat-building trade, the large 8-in. disk will remove material at an amazing rate.

An orbital sander removes material as the disc spins in a circular pattern. There are soft, hard, flat, and curved pads—all used with different techniques and for different jobs. Soft pads conform to curved surfaces, and curved pads will sand to a feather edge. Hard, flat pads sand surfaces flat. I use a variable-speed Milwaukee® with a special pressure-sensitive adhesive (PSA) foam pad. I also have

a buffing attachment for buffing out finishes.

A random-orbit sander works like an orbital sander, except the disc not only orbits but also rotates. The random action produces a sanding pattern that is almost indiscernible on the surface of the wood. On flat surfaces, this can save you from hand-sanding completely. But if you try to sand a curved surface or the edge of a project, the rotation of the sanding pad stops. Sanding anything but flat surfaces with a random-orbit sander defeats the whole purpose of using this machine.

ALWAYS HOLD IT STEADY AND FLAT. Some newer orbital sanders are as aggressive as belt sanders. As with any sander, the pad should be held flat on the surface. Any time the pad is tilted, it digs a crater in the surface of the work. Back up a grit or two to remove them.

Hand-Sanding With a Block

Always use a block when hand-sanding a flat surface. Without a block, hand-sanding applies pressure only where your fingers are, resulting in a surface that will never be as flat as you'd like. A block spreads the pressure evenly across the board. To apply pressure to the high spots on the board without loading up the paper, cushion the block with cork or felt. As the sandpaper cuts, the dust is deposited more evenly on the surface, not just in a few spots.

Do not use a hard wooden block for hand-sanding. The sandpaper almost immediately gets filled up in just a few spots. These spots then build up into small, volcano-shaped high points, and the result is a project that has scratches in it, even after all your hard work.

My sanding block is nothing more than a block of wood with felt glued on one side. I cut a block the right size, glue ¼-in.-thick felt on it, and that's it. I make my sanding blocks one-third the size of half of a sheet of paper and then glue on the felt. For sandpaper, I tear sheets in half, then fold this half piece into thirds (see the photo below). The entire sheet is used with this system. Folded in thirds, there is sand exposed on two sides. One side sands, the other goes against the block, sticking to the felt. When both of these sides are worn, refold the paper to expose the last third for the final sanding. This is one time where saving labor is worth more than the material. I only apply light pressure, and I change the paper often. Once paper gets dull, I throw it away and grab another piece.

For hand-sanding contours, a larger piece of sandpaper better fits my hands. The drawings below show an efficient way to use a whole sheet of sandpaper without waste.

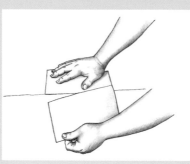

1. Sandpaper is creased but torn only halfway across its length.

2. First quarter of paper is folded with grit facing out.

3. The two thicknesses of sandpaper are folded onto sheet's third quarter.

FOLDED HALF SHEETS FOR A SANDING BLOCK. Tear paper in half and fold it into thirds, taking care to use every surface before you discard the sheet. Felt on the block evens out the sanding pressure and helps hold the paper in place.

4. Fourth quarter of paper is folded into final shape, without ever having to fold grit onto grit.

The microscopic grains of sand on sand-paper are initially very sharp. They cut into the surface quite readily with little effort or pressure. They soon dull, however. The sharp points break off, the paper gets clogged with dust and cutting no longer takes place—only rubbing. And this rub-bing has the effect of polishing or glazing the wood's surface, not smoothing it.

Sanding efficiently means going through a lot of sandpaper. It's a hard rule to get used to, but I save a great deal of time and sweat by throwing away sandpaper before it gets dull. You can feel the paper lose its

Flattening a Tabletop

Flattening a tabletop is one of the toughest sanding jobs, especially if your glued-up boards are not quite flush with one another. But the plan of attack is quite simple: Remove the high spots and avoid sanding the low spots. Here's the easiest way I've found to bring a tabletop flat.

1. First concentrate on the glue joints, because they will eventually be the low point to which you must work once they're flush. With a belt sander, I sand with 100 grit at about a 45-degree angle, first to the right of the grain pattern and then to the left. Sand evenly in both directions. This way there's a chevron pattern to the sanding marks.

2. & 3. Use a straight board as a batten and coat it in chalk to see where the top is not flat. Rubbing the board across the top quickly highlights the high spots where more sanding is needed.

4. Once you sand off all of the chalk, start the process over. Eventually, the piece will be flat. If this sounds oversimplified, it's not. Once the surface is flat, use the same grit to sand with the grain to remove the cross-grain scratches.

It's possible to do this flattening with a well-tuned and very sharp handplane using the same technique, but you risk digging into the work or causing tearout. On the other hand, for a few dollars, a commercial drum sander can flatten your tabletop in just a few minutes.

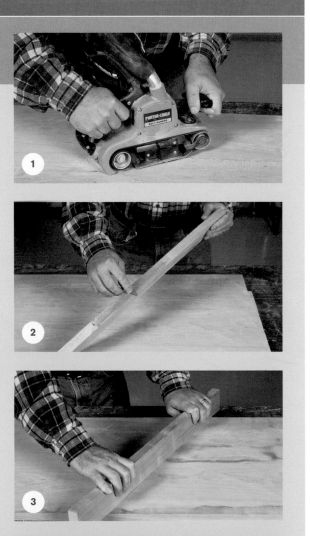

Virtually Dust-Free Sanding

The dust produced by sanding is the finest and probably the most harmful. Newer sanding tools collect more of the dust generated, but there are still a few ways to get even better dust collection. With portable sanders, I don't use the dust-collection bags. Instead, I increase the effectiveness of the internal vacuum system by hooking a vacuum hose directly to the sander.

My best defense is a shopmade downdraft table. There are commercial versions available, but I made a simple 2x4 frame and covered both sides with ¾-in. plywood. On one side, I cut a hole to accept hookup from a dust-collection system. I also drilled a number of small holes. The suction from the dust collection picks up stray dust through the holes and helps hold the project to the table.

PLIABLE SANDING BLOCK. The author glues sandpaper to ¼-in. plywood, which bends and slides smoothly over the surface, keeping a curve in line.

ROUNDING THE GLUELINES. Horizontal chalklines stripe the surface, and only the highest spots–the gluelines–are sanded in vertical stripes until the curve nears its final shape.

CHALKING HIGH SPOTS. A thin batten is coated with chalk, then bent across the surface to find high spots in the curve. The chalk marks are sanded away with a sanding block.

cutting action when sanding gets easier. This is because the paper is sliding over the surface instead of digging in. Use the oldest belt or disk until it is dull, then throw the old one out, and reach for a new one. That way you won't have 50 partially used sanding belts on the shelf.

The shadows left by glue may not be visible until the finish is applied, so around glue joints sand a bit more to ensure that the glue will be completely removed. I always try to err on the side of sanding too much rather than too little. When it looks like you're finished, sand just a little more.

If you're using a penetrating oil finish, you'll want the surface as smooth as possible, up to about 400 grit. But if you're using a water- or alcohol-based stain, the stain will

Fairing a Curve

Fairing a curve means shaping it to eliminate any lumps or hollows. In woodworking, as in sculpture, the only means you have to make the curve fair is to remove material. This means that you must concentrate on the high spots and leave the low spots alone. This sounds simple enough, but in practice it's sometimes difficult even to tell the difference.

Sanding just to be sanding almost always makes the curve more lumpy. On edge curves, I often see students attempting to smooth or fair a curved piece on the spindle sander by running the entire curve over the sander without stopping to feel the surface. I know they are about to have a bigger problem than they already have, so I stop them, with a reminder that sanding done sparingly and selectively will give them the result they seek.

The correct process is to sand the curve for only a few seconds, just enough to remove tool marks. Then run your fingers over the surface, feeling for consistency. When you find a high spot, mark it with chalk or pencil and remove only these lumps, staying away from the hollows as much as possible. Stop and feel the surface again, marking the spots in need of sanding as before. Gradually, the surface becomes smoother and the curve more fair.

Sometimes on larger curves, the lumps are hard to feel. You can find high spots by coating a batten (a flexible piece of wood) with chalk. Bend this batten across the surface and rub it back and forth. The chalk will rub off on the high spots, leaving a clearly marked area to sand.

A DOWNDRAFT TABLE KEEPS IT CLEAN. The author's sanding table is just a box drilled with holes to suck the dust away. This simple box, made of plywood and 2x4s, hooks up to a dust-collection system or shop vacuum.

raise the grain when it is applied, so stopping at 150 grit or 220 grit makes more sense. The first coat of finish sealer, paste filler, stain, or primer will harden and stabilize the surface.

Then move to the finer grits, from 180 to 400. Read and follow the instructions that come with the finishing materials before you start the sanding process. Let

the tools and sandpaper do the work. In no time, your project will be perfectly sanded and ready for finish.

LON SCHLEINING teaches woodworking seminars around the country and is the author of *The Workbench* (Taunton, 2004).

Taking the Spray-Finish Plunge

BY ANDY CHARRON

My first shop was a one-car garage. What space I had was filled with tools that were absolutely necessary to make furniture. That left out a dust collector and a finishing room. As a result, getting dust-free finishes was frustrating. Brushing on shellac and varnish worked fine for small projects, but as I took on bigger jobs and built more pieces, I turned to wipe-on oils because they weren't as fussy to use. Eventually, I needed more durable finishes that didn't take long to apply.

A spray system was the answer. Spraying on finish is fast and easy. You can get into places where brushes and rags are useless (see the photo on p. 40). Spray finishes look superb, too. The coating is more uniform and the finishes between pieces is more consistent. But once I was committed to changing to spray finishes, I knew I had some research to do.

Spray Systems and Finishes Are Better Now

The variety of spray systems has increased dramatically over the last 10 years. Manufacturers have introduced small, inexpensive units that are ideal for hobbyists and small shops. Also, there have been many improvements in high-volume, low-pressure (HVLP) spray systems, particularly in terms of transfer efficiency. The price of an entry-level HVLP spray system is around $200, and there's a wide variety of systems in the $200 to $500 range. These spray systems aren't much more expensive than many power tools.

Waterborne finishes have improved as well, and as a result, the need for dangerous, solvent-based finishes has decreased. Water-based finishes are nonflammable, which means that you no longer need a spray booth to get started. Having a clean spray area, a respirator, and good ventilation (I use an exhaust fan) will suffice. And a spray system won't leave you with a pile of oily rags that can catch on fire.

Brush-On and Wipe-On Finishes Are Slow and Exacting

In my furniture business, I brushed on varnishes for only a short time. Varnish was just too slow to brush and too slow to dry. And I needed excellent lighting to brush, sand, and rub out the varnish. I did stick with wipe-on oils for a while. Oil didn't require any special equipment, and I could oil in less-than-ideal conditions. I wasn't building up a thick surface film (like a varnish), so I worried less about dust and lint getting trapped in the film. Oil finishes soon became a key in my marketing strategy, too.

Most of my customers liked the phrase "authentic, hand-rubbed finishes."

Oil finishing does have drawbacks. The protection offered by an oil finish is minimal, and an oil finish needs more maintenance than other top coats. Surface imperfections, like scratches, stand out more than they would under a film finish. And oil finishes are time- and labor-consuming. Depending on the temperature and humidity, an oil finish can take several days to apply. It also involves a great deal of work. It's hard to get thrilled about rubbing out multiple coats of oil on 400 wooden clock frames.

Any Spraying Disadvantage Can Be Overcome

As attractive as spray finishing is (see the sidebar on pp. 40–41), it does have a few weaknesses. Setting up a safe, efficient system takes up shop space and costs money. Besides a gun, you will need a source of air (either a turbine or compressor), hoses, filters, and connectors. Because spraying releases finish mist into the air, you will also need a spray area that has fresh-air circulation. If you spray solvent-based finishes, you'll need to check with your local building inspector before you set up a booth. But if you spray

Spraying Has Benefits Over Other Methods of Finishing

1. Spray finishes are forgiving. Because a sprayed finish is built up in thin layers, small scratches and marks stay better hidden under a sprayed translucent finish than under an oil finish. Surface preparation is still important, though. This is especially true when spraying paints or opaque stains.

2. Spray finishes are fast. You can spray 30 stools or 1,000 small wooden blocks in an hour. And because the sprayer breaks the finish into small particles, each coat dries in a hurry.

Many varnishes, water-based products, and sprayed lacquers will dry to the touch in minutes. Some of them can be sanded and recoated in a few hours. Dust has a short time (while the coat is tacky) to settle on the work, which reduces the need for sanding between coats.

3. Spray finishes are versatile. Basically, any finish that can be applied by brush or by rag can be sprayed. If you use an explosion-proof booth, you can spray shellac, lacquer, and other solvent-based materials. If you don't have a booth, you can still spray water-based finishes. With some spray

SPRAYING GETS FINISH IN NOOKS AND CRANNIES. One reason Andy Charron switched to spraying is that it gets finish where other applicators won't. Here, he sprays water-based sealer on the latticework of a poplar headboard.

water-based products exclusively, you won't need explosion-proof fans and fixtures.

Unlike most brush-on and wipe-on finishes, spray finishes must be filtered and then thinned to the correct viscosity (see the photo on p. 39). Not thinning enough can lead to lumpy finishes and "orange peel." Using too much thinner creates problems, too, like drips and sags on vertical surfaces.

And it will take longer to build to the right film thickness. The result is you won't be able to get nice, glossy, clear coats, and paints won't hide the underlying surface or provide good color depth. Too much thinner also lengthens the drying time, so dust becomes a problem.

Finally, keeping your spray gun clean is critical. Although cleaning does involve some

SPRAY GUNS INCREASE PRODUCTION. Charron compares the number of clock frames he sprayed vs. those painted with a brush.

systems, you can apply water-based contact cement, which works great for laminate work.

4. Spray finishes can be precisely controlled. Spray-gun adjustments combined with proper spray techniques give you good control over how and where the finish is applied. A brush transfers nearly 100 percent of the finish to the work, but you have to be diligent at keeping the coat even and at the right thickness.

Even though the transfer efficiency of a spray gun is lower than a brush (between 65 percent and 85 percent), you can adjust air pressure, fan size, and fluid flow to ensure light, even coats. Also, because the atomized material flows together uniformly, there are no brush or lap marks.

5. Spray finishes are relatively easy to apply. Spray finishing is fairly basic. You can learn how to spray a simple case or frame in less time than it takes to master

brushing or wiping on a finish. With a bit of practice, you can spray stains and dyes to get uniform coverage and consistent color depth. After some more practice, you can use tinted clear finishes to do special techniques, such as shading or sunbursts. Because spraying allows a greater range of finishes, your projects will look more professional.

6. Spray finishes are consistent in quality. Without a doubt, the best reason for investing in a spray system is the overall higher quality of finish that you can achieve.

A spray-on finish is far superior to brush-on or wipe-on finishes. The problems caused by brushing, such as runs, drips, and air bubbles, are reduced with spray equipment. And brush marks are gone. You can spray an entire piece, no matter what its size or shape, with light, even coats of finish. –A.C.

effort and time, it doesn't take any longer to clean a spray gun than it does a brush.

Ultimately, Spraying Reduces Finishing Costs

Although some of the finish does get wasted through overspray, you can still lower your material costs. I've had to reject far fewer pieces that I've sprayed than those that were

finished by brush or rag. And spraying saves labor costs. In the first month, I more than offset the initial expense of the equipment (about $800). Now my business couldn't survive without a spray system.

ANDY CHARRON operates Charron Wood Products in Windsor, Vermont.

Which Spray System Is Right for You?

BY CHRIS A. MINICK

USE A BOOTH WHEN SPRAYING SOLVENT-BASED FINISHES, such as nitrocellulose lacquer. Here, the author uses a Binks high-pressure spray gun, which has a 1-gal. paint pot. These guns produce excellent results but lots of overspray.

Mention the names Delta®, General®, or Powermatic® to a bunch of cabinetmakers, and everyone in the group will know you're talking about woodworking machinery. Mention DeVilbiss, Mattson, or Sharpe to the same crowd, and you'll likely get some blank stares. Those companies are just three out of dozens that make spray-finishing equipment. Chances are, though, many woodworkers just don't know as much about choosing a spray system as they do about buying a tablesaw. Considering that a high-quality spray system costs as much as a decent tablesaw, it pays to be well-informed before you buy.

Andy Charron explains why he switched to spray finishing in his shop (see p. 38). I'll present some equipment options—high-pressure spray guns (see the photo at left), HVLP systems, and airless spray guns. But first, it would be helpful to know a little about spray-gun anatomy.

How a Spray Gun Works

The basic principle behind a spray gun is relatively straightforward. A stream of liquid finish is forced into an airstream, which breaks the liquid into tiny droplets (atomization) and carries them to the target surface. It sounds simple, but in reality, a collection of precision parts must work in concert to pull the whole thing off.

In a standard high-pressure system, air flows from the compressor hose through a series of valves and baffles in the body of the gun and out through an air cap. The valves and baffles control the maximum atomization pressure at the air cap. The volume of air used by the gun as well as the spray pattern is governed by the size and placement of the holes in the air cap (see the drawing on p. 45).

A standard air cap for furniture finishing produces a tapered (fan) pattern 9 in. to 11 in. long. Typically, the gun uses about 8 cubic feet per minute (cfm) of air at 50 psi.

Pulling the trigger extracts the needle from the fluid tip, which opens the orifice and allows the finish to enter the airstream. The size of the orifice and the viscosity of the finish control the amount of material sprayed. I've found that a 1mm orifice is ideal for finishing furniture. The fluid tips and needles are sold in matched sets (fluid setups). Most spray-system manufacturers have technical-service departments that will help you choose the right one.

Once the finish exits the tip, high-pressure air from the air cap blasts the stream into tiny droplets. The droplets can range from about 15 microns in dia. to 70 microns or more. The size depends on the fluid viscosity and on the equipment. Once the atomized finish is deposited, it flows together to form a smooth film. Generally, the smaller the droplets, the better the finish.

AN AIR COMPRESSOR CAN POWER a high-pressure or conversion-air HVLP spray system. With either type, you'll need an oil and water filter separator, a regulator, an air hose, and couplers. Choices for guns (from left): conventional touch-up, external and internal mix, two HVLP units, and conversion-air touch-up.

Gun composition affects the kind of finishes you can spray A gun that has an aluminum cup and fluid passages is compatible with hydrocarbon-solvent-based finishes like nitrocellulose lacquer and oil-based varnish. But within a matter of hours, the same gun will be corroded beyond repair if it is used to apply a finish that contains a chlorinated solvent, such as methylene chloride (which is the main ingredient in many paint strippers). Even nonflammable solvent cleaner will corrode aluminum parts. Similarly, the alkaline portion of waterborne finishes can damage bare aluminum parts if the gun is not cleaned immediately after use.

As a corrosion-fighting alternative to aluminum, some low-cost units combine plastic cups and dip tubes with brass fluid-

TURBINE-DRIVEN HVLP SYSTEMS are compact, but the hoses are cumbersome. Both the two-stage Graco/Croix unit (left) and the Wagner® single-stage model spray efficiently and are portable.

AIRLESS SPRAY SYSTEMS WORK WELL with latex paint and most varnishes, but they don't apply other finishes well. If not the right viscosity, the finish will be poorly atomized and leave a coarse, blotchy surface.

High-Pressure Spray Equipment

Early in this century, high-pressure spray equipment was developed in response to the automotive industry's need for high-speed finishing. Spray components have changed little since that time. A full system consists of three main parts: a compressor (with attendant hoses, tank and pressure regulator), an oil and water separation device, and a spray gun.

The air compressor is the heart of the spray system; both the horsepower rating and tank size affect spray performance. A 3-hp compressor with an air output of 10 cfm and a 20-gal. air tank is really the minimum size.

When air is compressed, water vapor in the air condenses to a liquid. If not removed, the water that passes through the spray gun will cause all kinds of finishing problems. So an oil and water separator is a critical part of any compressor-driven spray system. The separator also removes residual oil that's used for lubrication of the compressor.

Internal mix or external mix High-pressure spray guns are available in two types: internal and external mix (see the photo and drawings on p. 45). The mix designation is based on where the airstream is introduced into the fluid stream.

handling parts. But brass wears quickly, particularly if the gun is used to spray pigmented finishes like paint. The pigments act like the abrasives used in sandblasters.

Mild-steel components (especially fluid tips and needles) are also common in inexpensive spray guns. Though steel is compatible with most finishes, it has a nasty tendency to rust. One solution is to buy a gun that has a stainless-steel cup and fluid-handling parts, but that type is pricey. Those guns make sense for industrial users, but they are overkill for small shops. As an alternative, some spray guns come with stainless-steel fluid passages and a Teflon®-lined aluminum cup. The Teflon lining protects the cup from corrosion and makes for easy cleanup.

Air Caps

GUNS CAN BE INTERNAL MIX (LEFT) OR EXTERNAL MIX (RIGHT). The spring, retaining ring, and baffle have been removed in the external-mix gun.

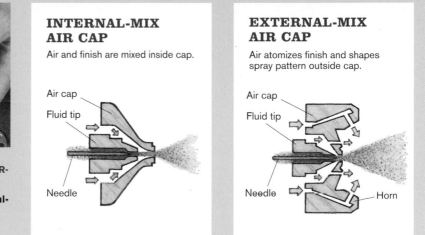

INTERNAL-MIX AIR CAP

Air and finish are mixed inside cap.

Air cap
Fluid tip
Needle

EXTERNAL-MIX AIR CAP

Air atomizes finish and shapes spray pattern outside cap.

Air cap
Fluid tip
Needle
Horn

Most internal-mix guns (air and fluid are mixed inside the air cap) produce a coarsely atomized spray. Although this spray is unsuitable for applying lacquers or other fast-drying finishes, it is ideal for applying thick, difficult-to-spray materials, like adhesives and pore fillers. Internal-mix guns consume modest amounts of air and can be powered with a 1-hp or 2-hp compressor. But they are limited to spraying slow-drying varnishes and paints.

By contrast, external-mix guns (air and fluid are mixed outside the air cap) are versatile. They're the most common spray guns used in woodworking shops. Hundreds of fluid-tip/needle/air-cap combinations are available to allow the spraying of virtually any liquid at almost any pressure. External-mix guns can be fed from a 1-qt. siphon cup attached to the gun or pumped from a 1-gal. remote pressure pot when greater quantities are needed.

External-mix spray guns have two drawbacks. They use lots of air, so they require at least a 3-hp (4 hp or 5 hp is preferable) compressor. And they aren't very efficient at putting the finish on the work.

Only about 35 percent of the finish actually lands on the target; the rest ends up as overspray. High-pressure spray guns only make sense in a shop that has a good spray booth.

More Finish Ends Up on Your Project With HVLP

HVLP spray equipment has been around a while. In the late 1950s, I painted models and birdhouses with an HVLP painting attachment that came with my mother's canister vacuum cleaner. HVLP equipment is more sophisticated now, but the underlying concept remains unchanged. To atomize the finish, HVLP systems use high volumes of air rather than high pressure. Unlike conventional spray guns, HVLP guns produce a soft spray pattern. The benefits are increased transfer efficiency, low overspray, and almost no bounce-back. Simply put, HVLP spray guns put more finish on the project and less on everything else in the shop and in the environment.

Spray-equipment manufacturers have taken two very different approaches to HVLP. Some have developed turbine-driven systems and others have developed

Considering that a high-quality spray system costs as much as a decent tablesaw, it pays to be well-informed before you buy.

conversion-air HVLP systems, which are driven by a standard air compressor.

Turbine-driven HVLP spray systems are portable Turbine HVLP systems use a fan (like those used in vacuum cleaners) to generate from 45 cfm to 110 cfm of air at pressures between 2 psi and 7 psi. You can buy turbines in three power levels: one, two, or three stage. The top photo on p. 44 shows a two-stage turbine and a single-stage unit. Each stage, or fan section, in the turbine adds approximately 40 cfm and 2 psi of air output.

Unlike a compressor, a turbine blows out a continuous stream of warm, dry air at a constant pressure. This eliminates the need for pressure regulators and air dryers (separators). But warm air can be a problem. The metal handles of some spray guns can get uncomfortably hot.

Also, dried drops of finish tend to accumulate on the fluid tip; eventually, the finish glob breaks free and deposits itself on the freshly sprayed surface. On the positive side, turbine systems are compact, store easily, and operate on 110v current.

The more stages a turbine has, the wider the viscosity range of the spray finish. When I sprayed with a one-stage turbine (a Wagner Finecoater), I had to thin the finish to get proper atomization. Thinning is the kiss of death for some waterborne finishes. When I sprayed the same finish with a two-stage turbine (a Graco/Croix CX-7), there was sufficient power to spray without thinning. I didn't try a three-stage turbine. Designed for multiple guns and high production, they're a bit pricey for me.

Conversion-air HVLP spray systems are versatile Conversion-air HVLP systems convert compressed air (under high pressure) to a high volume of air (at low pressure) by passing it through baffles and expansion chambers in the gun body. Conversion-air guns have the reputation of

being air hogs. But the latest conversion-air spray guns will operate off most 3- or 4-hp compressors. If your shop already has a compressor, it may power a conversion-air HVLP gun.

A big advantage that conversion-air systems have over turbines is that the atomization pressure at the air cap can be adjusted (between 2 and 10 psi with most guns) to accommodate a wide range of coating viscosities. I compared the two types of HVLP systems side by side (see the sidebar on the facing page). The conversion-air system consistently produced a finer atomized finish, a higher delivery rate, and a noticeable decrease in overspray.

Conversion-air spray guns work best when connected to ⅜-in. air hoses. The quick-connect fittings on the hose and the spray gun must be matched (connectors are available at most auto-paint and compressor repair shops). Use a ⅜-in. coupler; a ¼-in. coupler will negate the advantage of the larger hose.

Airless Spray Systems

Airless systems usually are associated with house painting rather than furniture finishing. But airless spray systems are common in large furniture factories. These commercial units operate at pressures approaching 4,000 psi. However, high pressure, high delivery, and high efficiency come with a high price tag.

Consumer-sized airless units (see the bottom photo on p. 44) still have a place in the shop. I like them for applying latex paint and oil-based varnish on certain projects. The motor size of an airless gun determines its price and its versatility. A 110-watt gun is powerful enough to spray unthinned latex paint. But with a 45-watt unit, the paint has to be thinned significantly. A motor rating of 85 watts or more usually is adequate for spraying furniture.

Evaluating Spray Patterns

I couldn't resist comparing the performance of the spray systems in this chapter. I used a gloss, water-based lacquer (tinted black) in each spray gun. This is a demanding test when you consider I didn't adjust the viscosity. Spray patterns reveal where atomization was poor (large spots on borders) and where fan adjustments were limited (wide dispersion band). In general, high-pressure and conversion-air HVLP systems delivered fine atomization and more uniform spray patterns. Turbine HVLP and airless systems produced coarser spray patterns. —C.M.

FINE AND UNIFORM

CONVENTIONAL HIGH-PRESSURE SPRAY (from Cal-Hank touch-up gun).

CONVERSION-AIR HVLP SPRAY (from DeVilbiss® touch-up gun).

COARSE AND SPLOTCHY

TURBINE HVLP SPRAY (from Graco/Croix gun). Finish was thicker than recommended viscosity.

AIRLESS SPRAY (from Wagner gun). Finish was thinner than recommended viscosity.

Unfortunately, airless spray guns produce a coarse spray pattern. So only slow-drying paints and varnishes should be applied with them. Lacquers, including waterborne varieties, tend to dry before the droplets flow together. The result is a rough texture (orange peel).

Even with these limitations, however, an airless spray system can help get you started spray finishing—and for a reasonable price. One of the best things about an airless spray unit is that it doesn't use a cumbersome air hose. It just needs an extension cord.

The Choice Is Yours

If you're considering a spray system for your shop, take a good, hard look at conversion-air HVLP spray systems. As a bonus, you'll have an air compressor to do other things in the shop.

CHRIS A. MINICK is a consulting editor to *Fine Woodworking* magazine.

Turbine HVLP Sprayers Keep Getting Better

BY CHRIS A. MINICK

UNLIKE CONVENTIONAL HIGH-PRESSURE SPRAY GUNS that hook up to large-volume compressors and are sold separately, **HVLP sprayers** are sold as complete units consisting of a gun, a turbine, and an air hose.

My mother bought a new vacuum cleaner about 45 years ago. Packed in the box with the accessories was a crude, plastic spray-gun attachment. The gun attached to one end of the vacuum-cleaner hose that was also mounted to the blower of the vacuum-cleaner motor. One afternoon when Mom was out of the house, I dragged her new vacuum cleaner to the basement and spray-painted several of my model airplanes. I didn't know it at the time, but this was my first experience with HVLP spray equipment.

HVLP technology may have remained that simple had it not been for the South Coast Air Quality Management District (SCAQMD) in Los Angeles. For decades, high-pressure, compressor-driven spray equipment was the only game on the block. The equipment is extremely versatile, spraying anything from water-thin liquids to molasses-thick paste. However, this versatility comes at a price: The spray gun must be tethered to a large, high-output, high-pressure compressor. Also, the transfer efficiency—a measure of how well the gun delivers the finish—of these spray guns is notoriously bad.

In the early 1980s, SCAQMD and other air-quality agencies across the country enacted stringent regulations that require spray guns to have transfer efficiencies of 65 percent or higher, running at air pressures of 10 psi or less. High transfer efficiency and low overspray translate into more coating on the project and less in the air—better for the sprayer operator and the environment.

To comply with the new regulations, companies developed two distinctly different spray-gun systems. Manufacturers of high-pressure sprayers, such as Binks® and DeVilbiss®, modified their basic high-pressure guns, creating one that converts high-pressure, compressor-supplied air to low-pressure (10 psi or less) air at the air cap. This type of gun, for obvious reasons, is known as a conversion HVLP spray gun. The original conversion guns met all regulatory requirements, but they were tremendous air hogs. Consuming air at a rate of 20 cu. ft. per minute (cfm) or higher, just one spray gun required a 10-hp compressor. Large shops could accommodate conversion guns, but small, custom shops did not have the air power to run them.

To answer that market need, the turbine HVLP spray gun was born. In this system a small, high-output blower (the turbine) supplies a high volume of low-pressure warm air through a fairly large-diameter hose. Each component—turbine, hose, and spray gun—plays a critical role in the overall performance, which is why turbine HVLP sprayers are sold as a complete system rather than as individual components. These compact, self-contained, portable spray systems are increasingly popular with woodworkers, especially as the prices continue to drop. I looked at five HVLP turbine systems that sell for under $500*. Here I'll share the results of my tests and give you some tips on selecting a system that will work for you.

THIS SPRAYER RUNS ON HOT AIR, TOO. **Since 1938, some vacuums have come with a spray-gun attachment.**

Compact, Self-Contained, and Portable

TURBINE-POWERED HVLP SPRAYERS are driven by high-speed compression fans that rotate at about 20,000 rpm. Each fan is called a "stage." In general, the more stages, the more varieties and thicknesses of finish the unit can spray.

HVLP TURBINES are smaller than most compressors. This unit weighs less than 13 lb. and is less than 12 in. high.

THE LIMITING FACTOR for HVLP systems is the amount of atomization pressure at the tip of the gun. A gun with only 2.8 psi, for example, cannot spray undiluted conversion varnish.

HVLP GUNS have larger passageways than high-pressure guns used with compressors to accommodate the higher volume of liquid moving through the gun under lower pressure.

UNLIKE HIGH-PRESSURE GUNS that use a fan-pattern knob to adjust spray, the spray pattern of HVLP guns is adjusted by moving the air cap in and out.

FLEXIBLE, LARGE-DIAMETER air hose gets the air to the gun.

ALL HVLP GUNS—and some high-pressure guns—are pressure-fed: The liquid in the cup is kept under constant pressure rather than fed by siphon. High-solid, water-based finishes work better in pressure-fed guns.

WHAT TO LOOK FOR BEFORE YOU BUY

Most stores will let you check out an HVLP sprayer before you plunk down your cash. Here are six things to look for:

1. Check the atomization pressure at the spray gun's tip with an inexpensive pressure gauge: 2 psi is the minimum required to spray most finishes successfully.

2. With the turbine running and gun attached, check air-hose flexibility. You should be able to maneuver the gun into tight spaces without straining your arm and without the hose getting in the way.

3. Measure the air temperature at the end of the hose with the gun detached. Temperatures higher than 120°F tend to clog the nozzle and air cap, especially with water-based finishes.

4. Inspect the spray-gun air cap. It should have clean air holes and a smooth surface.

5. Smell the air exiting the gun. Vapors from the plasticizers used in the manufacturing of the air hose may be irritating.

6. Inspect the spray-gun cup for corrosion; don't buy a corroded cup.

Turbines Drive the Air Supply

Turbine, in HVLP vernacular, is a fancy term for a vacuum-cleaner motor. Motors manufactured by the Ametek Lamb Electric Co.® propel the majority of HVLP systems produced in North America. The motors drive small, high-speed compression fans. Turbines are rated by the number of fans—called stages—attached to the central motor shaft. Single-stage turbines have one fan, two-stage turbines have two fans, etc. More stages translate to higher airflow and higher air pressure at the spray gun. You might reason that the airflow figures would be a good way to compare turbine power of different HVLP systems, but this is not necessarily true. I found the air-output ratings in the manufacturers' literature to be practically useless for comparison purposes. For example, the air output for the Apollo 700, a two-stage unit, is rated at 112 cfm while the output for the Lemmer T-55, another two-stage unit, is rated at 55 cfm. According to the Ametek Lamb data sheets, the outputs should be almost identical.

I talked with an airflow engineer to find out how to determine accurate airflow values. Following his advice, I constructed a test chamber with a 6-ft. section of 6-in.-dia. heating duct and ran my own airflow tests. I borrowed a hot-wire anemometer—a device used to measure airflow—to measure the air output of each HVLP turbine at the end of the air hose and at the air cap of the spray gun. The results startled me. According to my measurements, Apollo's air-output values dropped 80 percent, to 23 cfm, when measured at the end of the hose and to 11 cfm when measured at the spray gun. However, the Apollo unit was not alone. I concluded that all of the manufacturers in this test dramatically overstated the air output of their respective turbines (see the chart on p. 54). Clearly, air-output

numbers published in the manufacturers' literature are of little value to the consumer. But fortunately, airflow figures don't mean as much as the atomization pressure, which is the real key to successful spray finishing. Atomization pressure at the spray gun is the best measurement to use to compare turbine HVLP spray systems. Best of all, you can check it in the store before you lay your cash on the line. All you need is an accurate pressure gauge that will measure from 0 psi to 10 psi.

I purchased a fuel-pump gauge at an auto-parts store for $15 and used it to measure the air pressure at the end of the supply hose and the atomization pressure at the air cap on the spray gun. Once again, I found little correlation between my measured pressures and the manufacturers' published atomization pressures. On average, my figures were about a third less than those claimed by each manufacturer. The notable exception was Lemmer, which actually understated the atomization pressure on its model T-55 gun by about a third. The difference between 4.25 psi and 2.8 psi may not sound like much, but it makes a big difference in gun performance. To put these numbers in perspective, at 4 psi you can spray an undiluted conversion varnish; at 2.8 psi you cannot.

The fans in a typical HVLP turbine rotate at about 20,000 rpm. That much speed generates a lot of heat, warming the air supply to the gun. As far as I can tell, warm air is more of a nuisance than a benefit. Some manufacturers claim that the heat helps the finish flow out better, but I doubt the finish is in the airstream long enough to warm up appreciably. However, the warm air does heat up the air cap and the fluid nozzle, drying out and eventually clogging the gun with any overspray that may land on those parts. This is not a serious spraying problem; it's just a cleanup

AMERICAN TURBINE AT 950
Price: $495*

Pros
The AT 950 is the most compact, portable system of those tested. The gun is made of metal, and the system has an air-reducing valve to regulate atomization pressure.

Con
The air hose is slightly stiff.

CAMPBELL HAUSFELD® HV 3000
Price: $399*

Pros
The HV 3000 has a convenient built-in hose-storage rack on the turbine, and an interchangeable fluid nozzle and fluid needle are supplied. The system also has an air-reducing valve to regulate atomization pressure.

Cons
The air hose on the HV 3000 is located at the top of the gun, making the unit awkward to use. The trigger is located too far forward for comfortable use, and a squared-off grip adds to the discomfort. The air hose spews a high concentration of plasticizer vapors during use. The air cap causes an irregular spray pattern, and the gun produces a large volume of overspray. Overall, the unit has poor transfer efficiency. The spray-gun cup of the unit tested was corroded out of the package.

LEMMER T-55
Price: $375*

Pros
The T-55 is an extremely comfortable sprayer to use, and it comes with a well-written, informative instruction manual. Of the units tested, the T-55 has the best turbine filtration. The sprayer comes with a viscosity drip cup and is equipped with a 14-ft. power cord.

Cons
The T-55 has a slightly stiff air hose and no air-reducing valve.

APOLLO 700
Price: $499*

Pros
The 700 is the most comfortable sprayer to use. It has an extremely flexible air hose, filters are easy to replace, and the plastic handle stays cool during use.

Cons
On the downside, the 700 has no air-reducing valve to regulate atomization pressure, and it produces a spray pattern that's not elliptical. Also, I found the manual to be poorly written.

WAGNER® 2600
Price: $499*

Pros
The 2600 is a well-balanced sprayer with an industrial-quality, nonbleeder gun. The sprayer has a flexible rubber air hose, which makes the unit easy to maneuver. The system has an air-reducing valve to regulate atomization pressure and achieves very fine atomization. The 2600 had the least amount of overspray in the test. For convenience, the spray gun is stored in the turbine housing.

Con
The only problem with the 2600 is that it has small turbine filters.

TURBINE HVLP SPRAYERS

Models	Apollo 700	Lemmer T-55	Campbell Hausfeld HV 3000	Wagner 2600	American Turbine AT 950	
Turbine Info						**Air Output**
Amps	10	8	12.5	11	8	
Stages	2	2	3	3	2	
Diameter	5.7 in.	5.7 in.	5.7 in.	5.7 in.	5.7 in.	
Air Output						MEASUREMENTS OF ACTUAL AIR OUTPUT, made with an anemometer, did not agree with those of most of the manufacturers.
Per manufacturer	112 cfm	55 cfm	65 cfm	80 cfm	52 cfm	
Measured at hose	23 cfm	25 cfm	38 cfm	40 cfm	31 cfm	
Measured at gun	11 cfm	15 cfm	13 cfm	15 cfm	13 cfm	
Air Pressure						**Air Pressure**
Per manufacturer	4.5 psi	3.9 psi	6 psi	6 psi	4.25 psi	
Maximum	3.75 psi	3.5 psi	5.25 psi	5.75 psi	3.5 psi	
Atomization	2.8 psi	2.5 psi	4.25 psi	4 psi	2.8 psi	
Temperature						THE AIR PRESSURE at the spray-gun tip is what counts. A small difference in this atomization pressure can make a big difference in how well these systems work, especially with some water-based finishes.
Measured at hose	134°F	104°F	126°F	112°F	99°F	
Measured at gun air cap	114°F	88°F	115°F	84°F	85°F	
Spray Gun Info						**Temperature**
Type	Bleeder	Bleeder	Bleeder	Nonbleeder	Bleeder	
Hose connection	Handle	Handle	Top	Handle	Handle	
Fluid nozzle orifice size	1 mm	1.4 mm	General purpose	1.3 mm	1 mm	
Gun body (material)	Aluminum	Aluminum	Plastic	Aluminum	Aluminum	
Gun cup (material)	Aluminum/ Teflon	Aluminum	Aluminum	Aluminum	Aluminum	
Air-reducing valve	No	No	Yes	Yes	Yes	TURBINE SYSTEMS THROW out a lot of hot air. Some manufacturers assert that the warm air generated by the turbines causes the finish to flow out more smoothly—a claim the author disputes.
Transfer efficiency	60%	65%	50%	67%	69%	
Overspray	17%	14%	34%	11%	16%	
Atomization	Fine	Fine	Coarse	Very fine	Fine	

problem, especially on the units that generate higher temperatures. Still, if all else were even, I'd purchase the cooler outfit. After 10 minutes of operation, I measured the temperature with a dial thermometer.

Hoses Should Be Flexible

Crush resistance and flexibility are two things I look for in an air-supply hose of an HVLP system. Invariably, you will step on the hose while spraying, and a crushed hose will cut off the air supply at the gun. All units passed my crush test with flying colors. Hose flexibility is another matter.

A stiff hose makes the spray gun difficult to maneuver, which may result in a poor spray job. Apollo attaches a short length of highly flexible hose between the gun and the air-supply hose. This arrangement provided the best maneuverability and made it the most comfortable sprayer to handle. The Wagner unit is equipped with a heavy-duty rubber hose that provided nearly the same flexibility. The hoses of the other three sprayers felt a bit stiff by comparison.

Except for Wagner, all of the manufacturers provide plasticized vinyl air hoses with their sprayers. Vinyl hoses tend to stiffen as they age—especially at the elevated operating temperatures of these sprayers—because the vinyl emits the plasticizers that make it flexible. During normal operation, all of the vinyl hoses gave off an irritating smell. The concentration of plasticizer vapors spewing from the Campbell Hausfeld unit during my air-output tests was high enough to make my eyes water and my breathing difficult. I had to turn on a ventilation fan and leave the shop. By contrast, the rubber hose on the Wagner gave off no detectable smell.

Low-Pressure Guns Work Differently

Turbine-driven HVLP spray guns and conventional high-pressure spray guns look the same, but the insides are entirely different. The large air passages inside an HVLP gun make it beefier than a conventional spray gun. (I prefer the added bulk, because it fits my hand better.) But that's not the only difference between the two designs. The HVLP guns lack the fan-pattern adjustment knob commonly found on high-pressure spray guns. Instead, the fan pattern of an HVLP gun is adjusted by moving the air cap in or out, relative to the fluid nozzle. Unlike high-pressure guns, most HVLP guns are bleeder-type guns. Air flows (or bleeds) through the gun continuously, even when you're not spraying the finish. For that reason, I find bleeder guns bothersome. The constant flow of air stirs up dust in my shop, and the noise is annoying. Nonbleeder, turbine-driven HVLP guns, in which all airflow stops when you release the trigger, are usually found only on high-priced industrial spray systems. But to my surprise, the Wagner 2600 system comes with an industrial-quality, nonbleeder gun as standard equipment.

A basic tenet of spray finishing is that thinner finishes require less atomization pressure than thicker finishes. By keeping the pressure set to the minimum required to atomize a finish, you can greatly improve transfer efficiency and decrease the amount of overspray. To adjust atomization pressure on a compressor-driven sprayer, simply adjust the regulator. But turbine-driven HVLP systems don't have a pressure regulator. American Turbine, Campbell Hausfeld and Wagner have solved that problem by building an air-reducing valve into their spray guns. Slightly closing the valve to reduce atomization pressure at the spray tip improves the performance of these guns, especially when you want to spray thin finishes.

Spray Test of Three Finishes

I sprayed almost 6 gal. of finish (polyurethane varnish, nitrocellulose lacquer, and a spray-grade water-based finish) with the five HVLP systems I looked at. None of the units had trouble spraying any of the finishes. However, some systems performed better than others.

I was particularly impressed with the low overspray and fine atomization pressure of the Wagner 2600. The American Turbine AT 950 and Lemmer T-55 were close second choices. I had trouble adjusting the needle-packing gland on the Apollo 700 spray gun, and I never did get it adjusted to my complete satisfaction. Either the packing was too tight, which prevented the needle from stopping the fluid flow, or it was too loose, and finish dripped onto my hand.

The Campbell Hausfeld HV 3000 produced a coarse spray that left noticeable orange peel on the sprayed surface. It also left heavy stripes in the finish because of a poor air-cap design.

Unfortunately, the HVLP sprayer industry does not adhere to any standard test methods for evaluating spray-gun performance. Each manufacturer develops its own spray tests, which makes it difficult to compare systems based on manufacturers' claims. To determine how well these systems lived up to the claim of high transfer efficiency and low overspray, I conducted a series of quasi-scientific tests in my shop.

High transfer efficiency and low overspray are the hallmarks of HVLP sprayers. I've seen claims of 90 percent transfer efficiency for some industrial

sprayers. It may be possible to achieve 90 percent transfer efficiency if you spray only the center of a large, flat panel, but few of us rarely have to do only that—we finish three-dimensional furniture.

For my tests I built three plywood boxes, 24 in. long by 12 in. wide by 10 in. high, to simulate a piece of furniture. By weighing the spray gun and the boxes before and after each test, I was able to calculate the transfer efficiency. I tested each HVLP unit three times, then I averaged the results to arrive at the transfer efficiency shown in the chart on p. 54. To keep things fair, I sprayed the same finish with each gun after adjusting each one to produce a 6-in. spray pattern. I was surprised at the high transfer efficiency achieved by all of the units I

Look for an air cap with clean, crisp holes and a smooth surface.

WHICH AIR CAP DELIVERS a better finish? A well-machined air cap, such as the Lemmer (left), had a more efficient spray pattern with less overspray than the Campbell Hausfeld cap (right).

tested. A 69 percent transfer efficiency is great in anybody's book.

Overspray and atomization are more subjective measures. Overspray means different things to different finishers. To me, overspray is that small amount of finish that falls back onto the sprayed surface, giving a rough texture to the finished piece. To evaluate this elusive but important parameter, I placed a grid over the test spray pattern and simply compared the number of squares inside the central spray pattern to the total number of squares with finish in them. Simple division yielded a percentage. Although this test may not be absolutely accurate, the overspray values I calculated reflect what I observed in my spray booth. Overspray of 20 percent or less is acceptable in most cases. Atomization is a purely arbitrary value based on my spraying experience with high-pressure and other HVLP systems. Very fine atomization is similar to that of a high-pressure gun; coarse atomization is not suitable for furniture finishing.

To compare the test sprayers with standard high-pressure equipment, I conducted the same series of tests with my Binks model 95 high-pressure spray gun. My trusty Binks was the hands-down winner of the atomization contest, but it exhibited a miserable 42 percent transfer efficiency and an immeasurably high overspray.

The air cap has a major influence on transfer efficiency, overspray, and overall performance of any spray gun. A good-quality air cap will have clean, crisp holes in the air horns and a smooth surface without any bumps (see the photo at left).

How Does It Feel?

Not surprisingly, the handle design and air-hose placement affect the ease with which a spray gun is used. Simply put, the better it feels in the hand, the easier it is to use. The air hose connects at the bottom of the handle and hangs down toward the floor on the American Turbine, Apollo, Lemmer and Wagner guns. This arrangement keeps the hose out of the way and allows maximum maneuverability. The air hose on the Campbell Hausfeld connects at the top of the gun and points backward over the operator's arm. I found that design awkward to use, and it would clearly make spraying inside cabinet carcases especially difficult.

The handle design of the Lemmer T-55 made this gun feel like an extension of my arm. The trigger was comfortable and positioned perfectly, and the grip rested nicely in the palm of my hand. The Campbell Hausfeld gun was the opposite. It had an uncomfortable, squared-off grip, and the trigger was too far forward and dug into my finger. My hand hurt after spraying with the Campbell Hausfeld gun for an hour or so. Worse yet, when I first unpacked the gun, the inside of the aluminum cup was severely corroded and contained some unknown brown liquid. I checked two other Campbell Hausfeld HV 3000 sprayers at two different stores, locally, and found the same conditions on both.

★Please note price estimates are from 1999.

CHRIS A. MINICK is a consulting editor to *Fine Woodworking* magazine.

Vacuum Motor Turns into a Spray Rig

BY NICK YINGER

SHOP-BUILT SPRAY UNIT. A high-volume, low-pressure unit like this one that the author built is ideal for on-site work or in the shop.

For years, I did my spray finishing with a conventional compressor-driven setup. I was never entirely satisfied with the arrangement, and I recently built my own HVLP unit, as shown in the photo at left, to replace it. What bugs me about conventional spraying? For starters: finishing the inside of a case with a swirling cloud of overspray billowing back in my face. I can't see what I'm doing, and I wind up ingesting a big dose of chemicals no matter what kind of mask I wear. Even when I'm spraying water-based finishes, which are inherently safer, I find overspray annoying. Although they're neither toxic nor flammable, water-based finishes are expensive, so it makes even less sense to blast these precious fluids all over the booth with air compressed to 50 pounds per sq. in. (psi). HVLP spraying looked like the answer to these problems. This method promised to transfer 70 percent to 80 percent of the material from the gun to the object compared with 20 percent to 30 percent with a conventional setup. To accommodate a stream of warm, dry, low-velocity air, HVLP guns have large hoses and air passages. They use copious amounts of air—as much as 30 cu. ft. per minute (cfm) but at only 5 psi. (For pros and cons of HVLP, see the sidebar on pp. 60–61.)

I had a 3-hp compressor, so it seemed a simple matter to install a large, low-pressure regulator to feed 5-psi air to the gun. But there was a catch. A 3-hp piston compressor won't pump 30 cfm continuously at any pressure. The rule of thumb is 1 hp per 4 cfm of air, and we're talking about large, healthy, industrial horses, not puny, under-fed, home-improvement horses. Because 8-hp to 10-hp compressors are expensive and connecting my small compressor to a tank the size of a submarine seemed imprac-tical, I decided I'd investigate the turbine compressors sold with HVLP guns.

I borrowed an HVLP unit from a friend and used it to finish some bathroom cabi-nets. It performed beautifully: almost no overspray, good atomization, and good fluid and pattern control. My only criticisms were that the hose seemed cumbersome, and the handle of the gun became uncom-fortably hot.

As I used the HVLP unit, I couldn't help thinking that if it acts like a vacuum cleaner, sounds like a vacuum cleaner, it must be a vacuum cleaner. I peeked inside. Sure enough—a two-stage vacuum cleaner turbine with an 8-amp motor! Soon there-after, I set out to build my own HVLP tur-bine compressor.

Build Your Own HVLP Unit

An HVLP machine is a centrifugal turbine compressor. It is contained in a box with an inlet to bring air into the turbine and a plenum or outlet chamber to capture the compressed air discharged by the turbine and route it to your sprayer hose (see the drawing on p. 63). The turbines used in large vacuum cleaners are integral with their electric motors and are referred to as vacuum motors.

First buy a vacuum motor Go to an industrial supply company, or get their catalog. I bought mine at Grainger℠ (see

"Sources" on p. 63); their catalog lists 45 vacuum motors, ranging from $40★ to more than $280. You'll find a wide selection of features, such as bearing type, motor volt-age, number of compressor stages, and motor amperage. Most important for this application is bypass, not flow-through motor cooling. This means the motor is cooled by a separate fan. With this design, the motor won't overheat if the vacuum inlet or outlet is obstructed.

Single-stage compressors move large volumes of air but produce the lowest pressure. Two- and three-stage units supply higher pressure air at some sacrifice in vol-ume but typically have more powerful motors and, hence, better overall perform-ance. I chose a two-stage turbine with a 13-amp motor rated at 116 cfm that costs $163, an Ametek model #115962. I could have purchased a less powerful unit, but I wanted to be able to operate two spray guns on occasion, and anyway, I like over-built machinery. For a one-gun setup, you might try the Ametek 115757-P, which costs $63. For the rest of the parts in my HVLP unit, including the hose but not the gun, I spent less than $70.

Make a cradle for the motor These motors are designed to be mounted by clamping the turbine housing between two bulkheads using foam gaskets. Make the rear bulkhead first. Cut it to size, bandsaw the circular hole, and then chamfer the back side of the hole. The chamfer will ease the flow of motor-cooling air away from the motor housing. Cut the positioning ring to size, and rough out the hole with the jigsaw, leaving it slightly undersized. I made a Masonite® routing template to exact size by cutting the hole with a fly cutter on the drill press. Use the routing template to finish the hole in the positioning ring.

Cut the housing sides, top, and bottom to size, and make the dado for the rear

With HVLP, far more of what you spray sticks to the object you're spraying.

Conventional Spraying vs. HVLP

BY DAVE HUGHES

OK...it's 8 A.M., and you've just entered your shop, coffee in hand. Standing before you is your latest project, nearly completed. It just needs to be lacquered. You take a deep breath, fill your spray gun, crank up the compressor, put on a particle mask and go for it. Fifteen minutes later, the atmosphere in your shop resembles that of Venus, every tool is covered with a fine white dust, the shop's out of commission for the rest of the morning, and you've got a serious headache. Sound familiar? If, like most of us, you've tried to do finishing with conventional spray equipment in a small shop space, it probably does. Well, there's an alternative. It's high-volume, low-pressure (HVLP).

By now, most professional finishers have an HVLP unit in their arsenal of tools and increasingly, the units are finding favor with folks who do only occasional finishing. One big reason is that HVLP units have far higher transfer efficiency than conventional spray units. This means, simply, that most of the stuff you're spraying goes where you want it to go. A painter friend of mine did his own little test when HVLP first hit the market. He painted one cabinet with a traditional, compressor-driven gun and an identical cabinet with an HVLP unit. When he was done, there was three times as much paint left in the HVLP cup. Where was the paint missing from the conventional gun? All over.

Aside from transfer efficiency, HVLP offers a string of clear benefits over conventional setups:

• They are compact, lightweight, self-contained, easy to set up and clean.
• The guns have a wide variety of spray-pattern settings for finishing intricate shapes as well as broad, flat surfaces.

bulkhead in each of them. Then drill the cooling outlet holes in the side pieces. Assemble the housing with the rear bulkhead in place, and when the glue has set, drop in the positioning ring, and glue it in place. I used screwed butt joints for the housing pieces and relied on the bulkhead to stiffen the box.

Gasket and sealant The turbine is held in the circular rabbet created by the bulkhead and positioning ring and is isolated from the wood by silicone rubber sealant. To hold the turbine centered in the rabbet while the silicone sets, cut three 2-in.-long pieces of $\frac{1}{8}$-in.-inside-dia. (ID) soft rubber tubing that compresses to about $\frac{1}{16}$ in. under moderate pressure. (This surgical tubing, with a wall thickness of $\frac{1}{32}$ in., is

HVLP IN A SMALL PACKAGE. At 15 in. sq. and 18 lbs., the shop-built turbine-powered HVLP spray unit in the photo at left is a fraction of the size and weight of the standard medium-sized compressed air setup in the photo at far left.

- The low-pressure air supply is adjustable and so creates far less bounce-back of material from inside corners.
- The dry, heated air helps materials flow on smoothly, level out nicely, and set up quickly. It also helps avoid blushing on cold, damp days.
- Your shop is not rendered useless for hours. (But open a window anyway.)

Drawbacks? There are a few:

- HVLP units are not really a high-production tool but are more suited for small to medium-size projects.
- Standard models have a rather cumbersome air hose all the way to the gun, limiting wrist mobility somewhat.
- As with any quart-gun arrangement, you can't spray upside down, and you're constantly, it seems, filling it

up. (Higher-priced models offer a 1-gal or 2-gal. pot that stands on the floor for less-restricted gun movement and less-frequent fill-ups.)

- And there's that whining motor—it reminds me of a car-wash vacuum.

HVLP is a definite advance for the small-shop woodworker or finisher who wants professional results. With prices starting under $500 and savings from high transfer efficiency, they're a good investment. From the money you save, stake yourself 50 bucks for a decent charcoal respirator and a pair of earplugs.

DAVE HUGHES is a professional finisher in Los Osos, California.

available in hobby shops and medical supply houses.) Lay the housing on its back, and put a generous bead of silicone in the rabbet. Lay the three pieces of tubing across the rabbet at 12 o'clock, 4 o'clock, and 8 o'clock, and push the turbine down into the wet silicone. If you want the turbine to be easily removable later, spray the rim with an anti-stick cooking spray such as PAM® before setting it into the silicone. Let the

silicone set, and trim off the squeeze-out and tubing ends later.

Next rout the gasket grooves around the front edge of the housing, and press lengths of ³⁄₁₆-in.-ID soft rubber tubing into them. Make the front and back covers, and apply the rings of ½-in.- by ½-in. adhesive-backed weatherstrip, as shown in the top photo on p. 62, and then screw on the front and back.

IMPROVING SPRAYER OUTPUT. Plastic laminate coiled in the outlet chamber acts as a fairing and increases output by lowering resistance. Weatherstripping and rubber tubing form gasket seals.

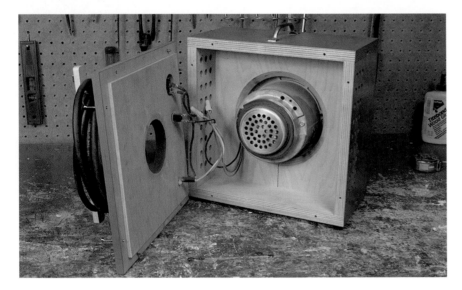

MOUNTING ELECTRICALS. Switch, cord, and circuit breaker are mounted in the back panel. Holes in the side of the back chamber are for motor-cooling air. A wooden cleat holds the wound cord.

Holes in the box I tried various locations for the outlet holes and found no detectable differences. But I did get better output when I installed a fairing made from a strip of plastic laminate, which makes the outlet chamber roughly cylindrical. Drill one or two 1-in. outlet holes in the housing, and screw ¾-in. pipe thread close nipples into them. Attach adapters to the nipples to provide ¾-in. male hose threads.

I attached a large shop-vacuum air filter to the front cover. Four short dowels hold the base of the filter in place, and a bracket pulls it tight against the cover. The bracket consists of two threaded rods screwed into the front cover joined by a hardwood crosspiece with a bolt through its center. A washer and wing nut secure the closed end of the filter against the crosspiece. You could also try using a large automotive filter. In that case, a Masonite or plywood disk secured by a similar bracket could hold the filter against the front cover.

Electricals Mount the electrical parts: a heavy-duty switch, a circuit breaker with the appropriate rating for your motor, and the supply cord through the back cover, as shown in the bottom photo at left. Then add rubber feet, a carrying handle, and a cord-storage device.

Nice hose I tried three different types of hose. All were ¾ in. ID and can be equipped with ordinary garden hose threaded fittings or quick-connect couplers. The most flexible was the lightweight, corrugated type provided with most factory-built HVLP sprayers, but its rough inner surface doesn't deliver as much air as smoother types. Plastic garden hose is cheap, smooth inside, and flexible when warm, but in use, the heated air causes the hose to become too soft and to kink easily. My favorite is Shields Vac extra heavy duty/FDA hose available from marine distributors. It is made of a soft, flexible vinyl molded around a hard vinyl helix. It's recommended by the manufacturer for use in boat plumbing below the water line, which means it will withstand a lot of heat as well as mechanical and chemical abuse.

Gun control You can't just hook up your old gun to your HVLP turbine. HVLP guns are designed to enable them to atomize fluids with low-pressure air. List prices for these guns start at around $250. Of the

SHOPMADE HVLP UNIT

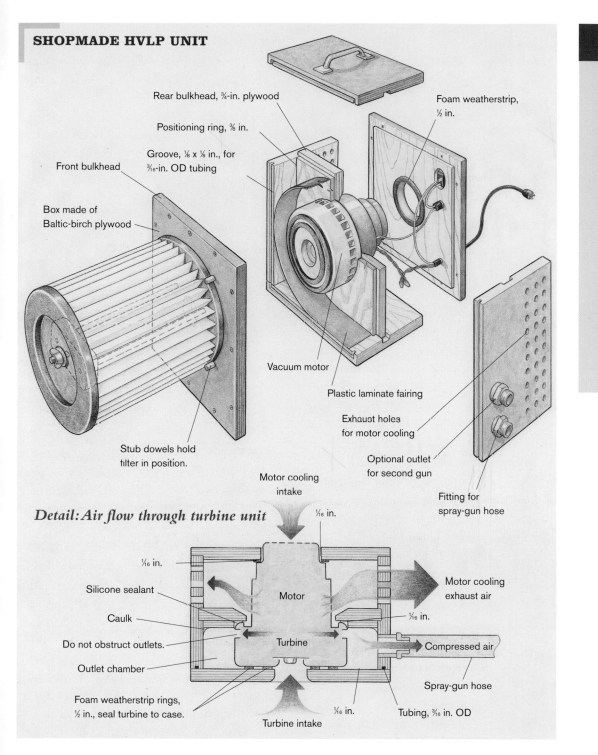

Rear bulkhead, ¾-in. plywood

Positioning ring, ⅜ in.

Groove, ⅛ x ⅛ in., for
³⁄₁₆-in. OD tubing

Front bulkhead

Box made of
Baltic-birch plywood

Foam weatherstrip,
½ in.

Vacuum motor

Plastic laminate fairing

Exhaust holes
for motor cooling

Optional outlet
for second gun

Fitting for
spray-gun hose

Stub dowels hold
filter in position.

Detail: Air flow through turbine unit

Motor cooling
intake

¹⁄₁₆ in.

¹⁄₁₆ in.

Silicone sealant

Caulk

Do not obstruct outlets.

Outlet chamber

Foam weatherstrip rings,
½ in., seal turbine to case.

Motor

Turbine

Motor cooling
exhaust air

¹⁄₁₆ in.

Compressed air

Spray-gun hose

Turbine intake

¹⁄₁₆ in.

Tubing, ³⁄₁₆ in. OD

Sources

Grainger
333 Nightsbridge
Pkwy.
Lincolnshire, IL
60069
800-473-3473
www.grainger.com

DeVilbiss
1724 Indian
Wood Cir.
Suite F
Maumee, OH
43537
800-338-4448
www.devilbiss.com

HVLP guns I've tried, my favorite is a DeVilbiss (see "Sources"). The current model most like mine is their JGHV 5285, which lists for $365. It has stainless-steel fluid passages and a stainless-steel needle, so water-based finishes won't cause corrosion.

And much to the relief of my palms, the handle is a nylon composite that doesn't get hot in use.

★Please note price estimates are from 1994.

NICK YINGER is a professional land surveyor in Kirkland, Washington.

Touch-Up Spray Guns

BY JEFF JEWITT

GRAVITY-FEED GUN

SIPHON-FEED GUN

Some woodworkers are addicted to power tools and collect routers. Others prefer hand tools and may have hundreds of planes or chisels. I have to confess an addiction to spray guns—I love them. At one time I counted more than 15 in my collection, and after selling half of them last year, the collection has grown into the double digits again. Out of all my spray guns, the one I reach for most often is a touch-up gun.

The touch-up gun is capable of jobs other than what the name implies. I routinely use these little gems for applying finishes to smaller projects, spraying stains, shading, and toning finishes and, of course, touching up finishes that need minor repairs. And because some of these guns are dirt cheap, I don't care whether I muck up one of them by inadvertently leaving something in the gun that I shouldn't, such as milk paint or catalyzed lacquer.

I often apply stains in more than one layer. My favorite first (or ground) stain color is a water-soluble dye stain. And I've found that there is no better applicator than a touch-up gun, particularly on large pieces where brushing on a dye stain can cause lap marks (see the top photo on the facing page). For a simple dye stain, atomization isn't critical, so I just use the gun to wet down the wood with a dye and then blot up the excess. For intricate inside areas, I can easily adjust the angle of the fan so I hit the corners first. I also cut back on the amount of air, so the vortex of the spray pattern doesn't prevent the dye from getting into tight corners.

Coloring sapwood to match heartwood is a snap with a touch-up gun. You can cut back on both the fan pattern and the amount of fluid to lay down a subtle line of color to match the sapwood to the heartwood. When I do this, I usually start by wetting down the whole area with solvent for the stain that I'm using—alcohol, water, or mineral spirits—to get a better idea of the color I need to use.

Shading and toning are typically done after the base stain colors have been applied. My favorite toner is made by adding dye to a finish, creating a translucent effect. It can be used for the overall application of color (toning) or a more selective application (shading). Most standard-size guns and touch-up guns can be adjusted for the fairly wide fan pattern you need to apply a toner, but shading is definitely best done with a touch-up gun. If you want to shade an edge molding darker, or add a bit of dark color around the perimeter of a drawer or a tabletop, the touch-up gun is your best finishing tool (see the bottom photo on p. 66).

It's rare that I ever finish a piece of furniture without encountering some sort of

APPLYING STAINS. With a touch-up gun you can apply stains fast and evenly. Here, Jewitt uses the gravity-feed touch-up gun with a plastic cup to spray a water-based dye stain on an oak bookcase.

Several Choices, Two Basic Styles

Touch-up guns are basically smaller versions of regular spray guns, but they're really available in only two styles: a siphon-feed, overhead trigger design and a gravity-feed version. Both styles are available in either conventional air-driven or HVLP designs, with the HVLP models priced a bit higher.

The most expensive siphon-feed HVLP touch-up gun costs about $200*, but you can get a conventional air-driven, Taiwanese-made, overhead trigger gun for less than $50. With the gravity-feed models, you can expect about the same price range. However, some of the gravity-feed models are available with adapters for airbrush bottles, which increase the versatility of these guns, particularly for touch-up work.

Touch-up guns can be a valuable asset to small shops. For one, they usually require only 4 to 5 cu. ft. of air per minute, which is a fairly small air demand that is within the range of almost any compressor. Also, the smaller size of touch-up guns makes them easy to maneuver in tight spaces and while putting a finish on small items. This is a real asset when you have to apply stain or a finish inside small cabinets.

THEY'RE SMALLER AND LESS EXPENSIVE. The standard 1-qt. cup HVLP spray gun at left sells for about $170, while the small HVLP touch-up gun on the right holds about ½ pint of finish material and sells for $80.

SHADING AND TONING. Before spraying a shading finish tinted with color, use a scrap of cardboard to set the size of your spray pattern.

problem, and one of the most common is rubbing through the finish and the stain when the job is nearly completed. If you have a gravity-feed gun with an airbrush attachment, you can literally "draw" some color or patch the finish on a particular problem area. If you don't have this attachment for your regular spray gun, the small spray pattern of a touch-up gun allows you to feather in finish or color so that it blends in invisibly.

When I do this, I take a piece of cardboard that's larger than the affected area by several inches on all sides and put a slit down the middle by raising my tablesaw blade up into it (see the bottom photo at left). This mask is taped or held over the spot that has been rubbed through, and then I use my touch-up gun to apply the missing stain. I let it dry, then apply some clear finish. But before that dries, I lift up the mask and gently spray several coats of clear finish in the correct sheen with the gun set for a small pattern. After the repaired finish is completely dry, I can blend or feather in the finish as necessary with 0000 steel wool.

★ *Please note price estimates are from 2002.*

JEFF JEWITT restores furniture in Cleveland, Ohio, and is the author of *Taunton's Complete Illustrated Guide to Finishing* (2004).

TOUCHING UP. A mask makes a cleaner touch-up repair. A piece of posterboard with a sawkerf cut through it limits the amount of stain and finish applied to an edge on which the color has been rubbed through and removed.

TLC for Spray Guns

BY ANDY CHARRON

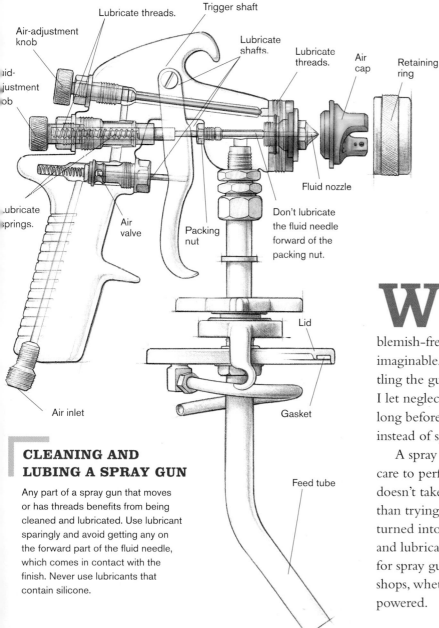

Lubricate threads.

Trigger shaft

Air-adjustment knob

Lubricate shafts.

Lubricate threads.

Air cap

Retaining ring

uid-justment ob

Fluid nozzle

ubricate springs.

Air valve

Packing nut

Don't lubricate the fluid needle forward of the packing nut.

Air inlet

Lid

Gasket

Feed tube

CLEANING AND LUBING A SPRAY GUN

Any part of a spray gun that moves or has threads benefits from being cleaned and lubricated. Use lubricant sparingly and avoid getting any on the forward part of the fluid needle, which comes in contact with the finish. Never use lubricants that contain silicone.

W hen I first began spray finishing, I was thrilled with how easy it was to lay down smooth, blemish-free top coats with any material imaginable. I was less thrilled with dismantling the gun and cleaning it after each use. I let neglect run its course, and it wasn't long before the gun protested by spitting instead of spraying.

A spray gun needs a little tender, loving care to perform well. The maintenance doesn't take that long, and it sure is faster than trying to remove built-up finish that's turned into an epoxylike glaze. Cleaning and lubrication methods are pretty similar for spray guns commonly found in small shops, whether they be HVLP or turbine powered.

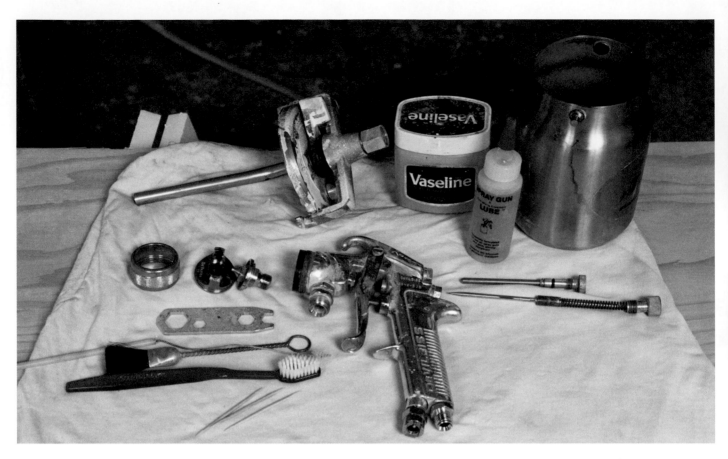

REQUIRED. **To get at places where finish tends to gum up a spray gun, partly disassemble it. Small brushes and wood toothpicks make good cleaning tools.**

Wood Toothpicks Make Good Cleaning Tools

Cleaning tools that come in contact with a spray gun should be stiff enough to remove gummy finish but not hard enough to damage the gun. Most gun manufacturers sell cleaning kits that include a skinny brush that fits inside hard-to-reach places. An old toothbrush works well, too. I also keep plenty of round wood toothpicks on hand for picking specks of finish out of hard-to-reach areas, like deep inside the horns of an air cap.

After washing out the cup, thoroughly clean the gasket that goes between the cup and gun (see the top left photo on the facing page). With a gravity-fed gun, the cup remains fixed; just remember to clean the cap and make sure the vent hole is clear.

Next, unscrew the air cap and look around for dried or gummy finish. This is where a wood toothpick will come in

handy (see the top right photo on the facing page). Don't use wire or metal materials because they can damage the gun. If the dried finish does not budge with the prodding of a toothpick, use a soft brush and lacquer thinner to dissolve the finish. Poor spray pattern or atomization often can be traced to a dirty air cap.

If your gun hasn't been thoroughly cleaned in a while, you may have to take it apart to get at gummed-up parts. A long, skinny brush dipped in lacquer thinner can be used to clean the inside of the gun (see the bottom photo on the facing page). Smaller parts can be soaked in lacquer thinner. But remove any rubber O-rings because lacquer thinner will cause them to swell. Although the O-rings will eventually shrink back to normal, you can damage them if you try to reassemble the gun when the rubber is swollen. Replace any O-rings that are torn or abraded.

CLEAN THE GASKET. The gasket needs to be free of debris; otherwise, the gun will not seal properly and will leak when tipped.

CLEAR THE AIR PASSAGES. Wood toothpicks won't damage the precisely machined air-cap orifices, which can get clogged with finish.

Special Steps for When You Switch Finishes

If you spray both water- and solvent-based finishes through the same gun, you need to take additional precautions. Water-based finishes can dissolve dried lacquer or lacquer thinner, just as lacquer will dissolve water-based finish left in the gun. The result is usually not pretty: A hunk of gunk splats on the tabletop as you make your last pass with the spray gun.

When switching from solvent-based finishes to water-based products, first clean the gun with lacquer thinner. Next, run denatured alcohol through the system, followed by water. When switching back, reverse the process.

Lube Anything That Moves

Cleaning a gun removes some oil from critical joints, so replace the lubricant regularly. The lubricant should be designed for spray equipment and contain no silicone. Silicone ruins finishes by creating depressions known as fisheyes. Once silicone has been

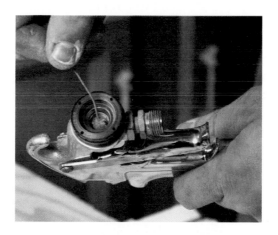

REMOVE THE AIR CAP AND FLUID NOZZLE. The inside of the gun is best cleaned with a skinny brush soaked in lacquer thinner.

introduced into your gun, it is difficult to remove, so be careful what type of lubricants you use both in and around your equipment. If you don't have spray-gun lubricant (available from paint suppliers), petroleum jelly will do. Don't get lubricant on the forward part of the fluid needle.

ANDY CHARRON operates Charron Wood Products in Windsor, Vermont.

A Low-Cost Spray Booth

BY JEFF JEWITT

Spraying a finish in a basement or a garage 25 years ago was risky business. High-pressure sprayers and flammable finishing materials were your only choices, and spraying these without proper ventilation was begging for a disaster. Not only did the risk of a fire or explosion loom large, but overspray was bound to settle on every horizontal surface in the immediate area.

With new HVLP spray equipment that drastically reduces overspray and with new water-based finishes, spraying finishes at home or in a small shop has become a viable option. One problem remains: how to ventilate the overspray. While water-based finishes are less problematic as fire hazards, the buildup of atomized finish and solvent can still be a health hazard. Spraying in an enclosed space without proper ventilation is unacceptable, so that leaves you with only a few options:

• You can spray outdoors. The problem with this alternative is that dust, bugs and other airborne debris will often ruin your wet finish. Also, strong breezes may prevent the atomized spray from landing where you want it.

• You can spray within a well-ventilated area, such as a screened porch. This is better because you minimize the possibility of debris landing on your wet finish, and the force of sudden breezes is reduced, but you still have overspray to worry about.

• You can spray in an enclosed area, such as a basement or a garage, and exhaust the fumes with a fan. However, basement windows are usually too small to fit a fan that will move enough air, and many garages don't even have windows. A small, portable spray booth solves these problems.

A Knockdown Booth May Be the Answer

Professional refinishers use specially designed spray booths to exhaust fumes in their shops, but these are quite costly, with prices starting at about $10,000* and moving upward, depending on all of the bells and whistles. These booths can also take up a large amount of floor space. The knockdown version I made can be built for much less (about $550). It can be set up easily in a garage or a basement with a large window and stored out of the way when not in use.

The heart of the ventilation system is an explosion-proof motor driving a nonsparking aluminum fan. (I bought one from a local Grainger distributor. It's rated at ¼ hp,

SPEND YOUR DOLLARS on an **explosion-proof fan motor.**

1,725 rpm, and it moves 2,000 cfm of air at 0 static pressure.) I recommend using at least a 16-in. fan and an explosion-proof motor, even with nonflammable water-based finishes. The fumes may not be flammable, but the fine dust that accumulates around the intake area and the discharge opening is a potential source of ignition. Check local electrical codes for making the proper electrical connections for the fan.

I mounted the fan in a torsion-box style assembly, which is fairly lightweight and plenty strong. I placed furnace filters in a slotted frame over the intake side of the fan to catch overspray. To the main center panel I added two lightweight wings, attached

with removable loose-pin hinges that direct the airflow toward the fan. They also help keep the assembly portable and more stable. A piece of cardboard or rigid insulation placed over the top significantly improves the efficiency of the airflow.

A hinged bracket on the outside of the middle panel keeps the assembly from tipping over while putting it together or taking it apart (see the bottom left photo). I also added a foil-faced foam shroud to direct the exhaust a little better. The booth should be placed so that the back of the fan exhausts into a large opening—either an open window in a basement or through the garage-door opening. To work efficiently, the

YOU DON'T NEED TO SPEND $25,000 on a spray booth. That's what it costs for the industrial-grade unit shown above, with air exchangers and installation included in that price. A small knockdown booth (left and on p. 71) is better suited for a shop in the basement or garage.

SMALL DETAILS MAKE FINISHING EASIER. A turntable (above) allows you to rotate a workpiece as you spray, which makes the job go faster and the results look neater. This technique is especially effective for spraying pieces that have many sides or odd shapes. A large, vinyl-coated hook to hang the spray gun (left) offers a safer, no-sparks alternative to metal-to-metal contact, and bright colors make it easy to locate.

amount of air the fan consumes through exhaust needs to be replenished. This make-up air is critical, and it can come from another open window or door to the room.

Small Accessories Add Big Conveniences

I use a simple 12-in. turntable that lets me rotate a workpiece as I spray. The turntable is made with steel bearings, and it's mounted between two scraps of plywood. By being able to spin a workpiece as I'm spraying, I can work faster and neater. For heavy objects, I can also mount the turntable on a cart with wheels, to move freshly sprayed pieces out of the booth easily.

I screwed vinyl-coated hooks on the sides of the panels to hang my spray guns. Vinyl is nonsparking, and it tends to hold metal parts a little better. Because of the weight of the hose, guns have a nasty habit of falling over if not hung up.

★ *Please note price estimates are from 1999.*

JEFF JEWITT restores furniture in Cleveland, Ohio, and is the author of *Taunton's Complete Illustrated Guide to Finishing* (2004).

Setting Up to Spray

BY JEFF JEWITT

GARAGE SPRAY BOOTH. The spray booth fits into a garage-door opening, and a box fan draws some of the overspray into the filter and fumes into the open air.

Low-Cost Fold-Away Spray Booth

The spray booth is made from three foil-faced rigid-foam insulation panels joined with duct tape. A removable top made from rigid-foam insulation helps keep the booth stable. A box fan draws air from the booth through a hole in the central panel. The hole is covered with a furnace filter.

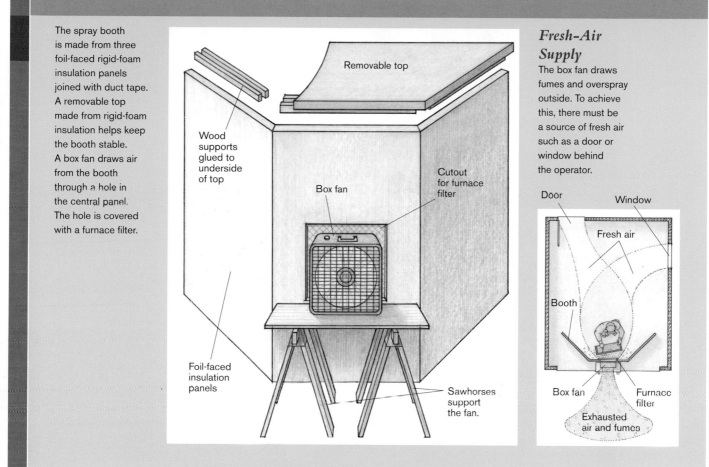

Removable top

Wood supports glued to underside of top

Box fan

Cutout for furnace filter

Foil-faced insulation panels

Sawhorses support the fan.

Fresh-Air Supply

The box fan draws fumes and overspray outside. To achieve this, there must be a source of fresh air such as a door or window behind the operator.

Door

Window

Fresh air

Booth

Box fan

Furnace filter

Exhausted air and fumes

Few woodworkers can afford a purpose-built spray booth, especially one that meets health and safety codes for spraying solvent finishes. At the other extreme, waiting for a fine day and spraying outside also is fraught with problems: The wind blows the spray back in your face, and every bug in the neighborhood dive-bombs the wet finish.

The spray booth and accessories shown here cost less than $200* and will allow you to spray indoors in a controlled environment. The booth is designed just for water-based finishes. I advise you not to spray flammable materials indoors unless you have a dedicated room outfitted with an explosion-proof fan and explosion-proof lighting fixtures.

Booth Controls Overspray

When spraying indoors, it's important to evacuate the overspray produced by the gun, not only for health reasons but also to prevent the atomized overspray from settling on your furniture and creating a rough surface. A simple approach is to construct a booth using three panels of foil-faced rigid-foam insulation joined with duct tape. Furring strips glued to a fourth panel form the top, which keeps the booth stable.

Spray-Finishing Aids

CONE FINISH FILTER. All finishes should be poured into the gun through a filter to remove impurities that might plug the gun.

AIR REGULATOR. This miniregulator is installed to set the air pressure coming into the gun.

INLINE AIR FILTER. Disposable filters trap water, oil, and other impurities coming from the compressor that would interfere with the finish.

LAZY-SUSAN TURNTABLE. A turntable allows you to spin the workpiece to finish all sides instead of walking around it.

GUN HOLDER. Gravity-feed guns need a special holder. This one includes a filter holder for straining the finish.

WORKPIECE SUPPORT. Nail boards can be made with nails or screws driven through a piece of plywood. Spray one side of a panel, then rest the wet surface on the nail board while the top surface is sprayed.

Cut a hole in the center panel about 30 in. off the floor. Slide a furnace filter in front of the hole, and rest a box fan on sawhorses on the outside. Use a cheap, open-weave filter; the more expensive kinds designed to trap minute particles will get clogged with finish too quickly. The 4-ft. by 8-ft. foam panels can be cut easily to fit any location, and when folded for storage, the booth is less than 2 ft. deep and light enough to be carried by one person.

Spraying Accessories

Unless you don't care about spray getting on the floor, lay down a cotton drop cloth. Don't use plastic sheeting because it becomes slippery when wet. Save large sheets of cardboard packaging to use for test spraying when setting up the gun or altering the fan pattern.

Drive multiple nails or drywall screws through a piece of cheap plywood. This nail board supports the work during and after spraying. Finish the nonshow side of the piece first; place that side on the points while you finish the show side. Because the workpiece needs to remain on the board while drying, you will need a separate board for each part you spray during each session.

A finishing turntable allows you to turn the workpiece instead of walking around it, and remain spraying toward the fan. A simple finishing turntable can be made by placing a 12-in.-dia. lazy-Susan swivel plate on a plywood base and then resting a nail board on top of the plate.

Place the finishing turntable on a pair of sawhorses to bring the workpiece up to a comfortable height and even with the fan for better fume extraction. For larger pieces, place the finishing turntable on the floor or rest the work on a dolly.

Spray-gun holders provide a resting place for the gun. Most cup and pressure-feed guns have a built-in hook and can be hung from plastic-coated hooks. Gravity-style guns require a gravity-gun filling station, which doubles as a convenient strainer support. Attach a piece of ¾-in.-thick plywood to the foam spray booth with construction adhesive, then screw on the gun holder.

To remove impurities from the finish, always strain it through a cone filter into the gun. A medium-mesh filter works best for most water-based clear finishes.

To prevent contamination from the compressor reaching the gun, invest in some inline air filters, which are available from auto supply stores.

You will require bright lighting in the booth to differentiate between wet and dry areas when spraying. I like to use halogen work lights on a tripod.

★ *Please note price estimates are from 2004.*

JEFF JEWITT restores furniture in Cleveland, Ohio, and is the author of *Taunton's Complete Illustrated Guide to Finishing* (2004).

Spraying Basics

BY JEFF JEWITT

It's a pity that so few woodworkers have taken the plunge and begun spray finishing. Lack of information is the main reason, and manufacturers bear much of the blame. Makers of professional spray systems assume you're already familiar with spraying, while the manuals for entry-level equipment give only basic details, and instructions on cans of finish tell you to consult your spray-gun manual.

To remedy this dearth of useful information, I'll describe the main types of spray guns and show you how to match the gun to the finish. By spraying various pieces of furniture, I can demonstrate the different spray strokes that will work best on each kind of surface. Together with "Setting Up to Spray" (p. 74), this information will allow you to begin finishing the way the pros do.

Match the Finish to the Gun

A spray gun mixes pressurized air and liquid finish in a process known as atomization. For proper atomization, it is critical to adjust the gun to the thickness, or viscosity, of the finish you want to spray.

Measure the viscosity of the finish A viscosity measuring cup is small with a precisely machined hole in the bottom. Most turbine-driven spray guns come with this type of cup, but owners of conversion guns can purchase one for around $10★. I use a Ford No. 4 cup, which is standard. If your cup is different, a conversion table is available at www.finewoodworking.com.

Viscosity is affected by temperature, so before you try to measure it, make sure the finish is at 70°F. Begin by submerging the cup in the finish, and then take it out. Start timing when the top rim of the cup breaks the surface of the finish. Raise the cup 6 in. over the can, and when the first break appears in the fluid stream, stop the clock. The number of seconds passed is the measure of the finish's viscosity (see the chart on p. 82).

Select the appropriate needle/nozzle Once you know the viscosity of the finish, the next step is to choose the matching-size needle/nozzle and sometimes air cap. Keep in mind that the different styles of gun (gravity, suction, or pressure feed) use

SELECT YOUR GUN, match it to the finish, and then practice the basic spray strokes.

Newcomers to spraying should use a HVLP spray system for the efficient way it converts liquid to droplets (atomization) and transfers those droplets to the object being sprayed.

TURBINE-DRIVEN HVLP

The first HVLP guns were powered by converted vacuum-cleaner motors, which evolved into two-, three-, and four-stage fans known as turbines. These HVLP systems offer a number of advantages to novice sprayers: They're normally sold as a packaged set, including the turbine, an air hose, a gun, and multiple needle/nozzle sizes for different finish viscosities, and generally come with good directions. Systems range in price from $300 to $1,000. You can get a good system for around $600.

COMPRESSOR-DRIVEN HVLP

If you already have an air compressor, you may want to consider buying a gun that will use the air from this source. Known as conversion guns, they convert the high-pressure air from the compressor to a high volume of low-pressure air at the spray tip. Prices range from $100 to $500, with good-quality guns available for less than $300.

Suction Feed

Air expelled through the front of the gun creates a venturi effect, pulling the finish into the gun. Although it's fine for medium- and low-viscosity finishes, this conversion spray gun can't pull up thick finish with enough speed to spray efficiently.

Gravity Feed

With the finish container mounted above the gun, this system lets gravity push the material down into the gun. Not only can you spray thicker materials more efficiently, but the gun also is easy and quick to clean. However, it is harder to get the gun into tight spaces.

Pressure Feed

You can pressurize either a cup attached to the gun or a remote pot that delivers the finish to the gun through a hose. The latter system makes the gun smaller and more maneuverable, but there are more parts to buy and clean.

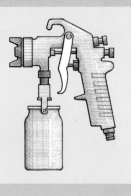

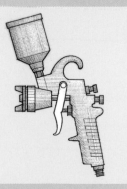

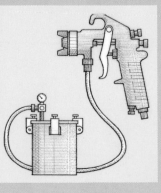

ANATOMY OF A SPRAY GUN

The components of most spray guns are the same as this typical HVLP conversion gun.

Fan-Width Control Valve

When the valve is closed, air is directed through the center and small annular holes of the air cap, resulting in a small, round spray pattern. Opening the valve lets air (blue color) into the outer horns of the air cap, which pushes the round pattern in from the sides, creating a flatter, elongated spray pattern.

Fluid-Delivery Valve

Adjusts the needle to control the amount of finish let through.

Air Inlet

The point at which air (blue color) is introduced into the gun.

Spring-Loaded Needle

Nozzle

Air Cap

Fluid Inlet

Where finish (red color) is introduced.

Plunger Rod

Opens a valve inside the gun that lets air through.

Trigger

Pulling back the trigger initially depresses the plunger rod, letting air flow through the gun. Squeezing the trigger all the way pulls back the needle, allowing finish to flow to the air cap. This compound trigger action ensures that the finish is atomized when it leaves the air cap.

Cheater Valve

Opens or shuts off the air supply.

different-size needle/nozzles for the same finish. Always use the smallest needle/nozzle that you can, as the smaller-diameter ones generally atomize finishes best. Try thinning the product before you select a larger needle/nozzle.

Some cheaper guns may come with only one size needle/nozzle, and in extreme cases the manual may not even specify what size needle/nozzle that is. In this case, you'll have to thin the finish until you achieve good atomization. Manufacturers of water-based finishes typically recommend thinning with no more than 5 percent to 10 percent of distilled water. Beyond that, you will have to use a viscosity reducer dedicated to

Setting Up to Spray

START WITH THE FINISH

MEASURE THE VISCOSITY. Submerge the viscosity cup in the finish and time how long it takes for the stream of finish to break.

VISCOSITY CHART

Generic finish viscosity	Viscosity time[a]	Appropriate needle/nozzle size[c]		
		Gravity feed	Suction feed	Pressure feed
Thin	10–15 sec.[b]	1.1 mm	1.3–1.4 mm	0.7 mm
	15–23 sec.	1.2–1.3 mm	1.5 mm	0.8–1.0 mm
	23–35 sec.	1.5	1.7 mm	1.1 mm
Medium	35–40 sec.	1.5–1.7 mm	1.9 mm	1.1–1.2 mm
	40–45 sec.	1.7 mm		1.2–1.3 mm
	45–55 sec.	1.9 mm	2.2 mm	1.3–1.5 mm
Thick	55+ sec.	2.2 mm	N/R	1.5–1.7

a = Measured in a Ford No. 4 viscosity cup with finish at 70° F

b Water = 10 seconds

c To convert millimeters to inches, mutlply the millimeter figure by 0.03937

CHOOSE THE RIGHT-SIZE NEEDLE/ NOZZLE. The higher the viscosity of the finish, the larger the needle/ nozzle to achieve good atomization.

FILTER THE FINISH. Strain the finish through a cone filter to catch impurities that could clog the spray gun.

that finish. Add the water or reducer in increments of 1 oz. per quart of finish until it sprays properly.

For the best finish "off-the-gun," it is a good idea to strain all finishes as you pour them into the gun. A fine- or medium-mesh cone filter works well to strain impurities from water-based clear finishes; a medium-mesh filter works for paint.

Create a Good Spray Pattern

Once you've matched the finish to the gun, make final adjustments at the gun. Also, select a respirator with cartridges suitable for the type of finish you will be spraying.

Setting up a conversion gun HVLP spray guns have a maximum inlet pressure of 20 psi to 50 psi; the exact figure is either

ADJUST THE GUN

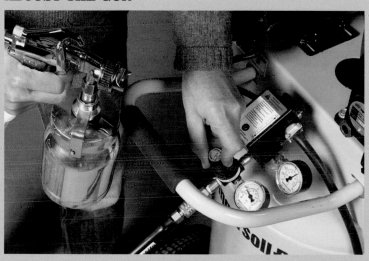

SET THE AIR PRES-SURE. With the gun's trigger depressed to allow only air to pass, set the outlet air pressure at the compressor, taking into account the hose-pressure drop (see the chart below).

HOSE-PRESSURE DROP

Inside diameter of hose	Pressure at compressor	Pressure drop		
		15-ft. hose	25-ft. hose	50-ft. hose
⁵⁄₁₆ in.	40 psi	1.5 psi	2.5 psi	4 psi
	60 psi	3 psi	4 psi	6 psi
⅜ in.	40 psi	1 psi	2 psi	3.5 psi
	60 psi	2 psi	3 psi	5 psi

Pressure drop is the amount of air loss from the compressor regulator to the gun's air inlet. For pressures below 40 psi, the pressure drops in the hose are negligible.

Dial in the Spray Pattern

The type of gun will determine the method of adjustment for the shape and orientation of the spray pattern.

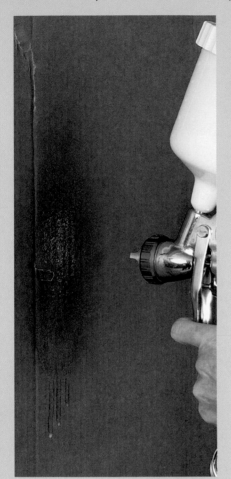

CONVERSION GUNS REQUIRE TWO ADJUSTMENTS. A valve at the back changes the pattern from circular to elongated. Twisting the air cap changes the orientation of the spray pattern.

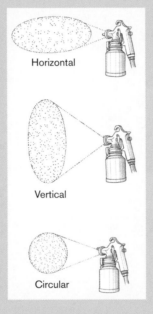

Horizontal

Vertical

Circular

Rather than alter the way you hold the gun, adjust the spray pattern to suit the object being sprayed. For vertical surfaces, a horizontal pattern gives optimum coverage; when spraying flat panels in the crosshatch pattern, adjust the gun to get a vertical pattern. A tight circular pattern reduces overspray when finishing narrow parts, such as slats and legs.

TURBINE GUNS ARE ADJUSTED AT THE FRONT. To adjust the pattern from circular to horizontal to vertical, just turn the air cap.

stamped on the gun's body or given in the instructions. Conversion, or compressor-driven, HVLP spray guns are designed to reduce this inlet pressure to 10 psi at the nozzle, enough to atomize most finishes. With the trigger of the gun slightly depressed to release air but not finish, set the compressor's regulator to slightly above this maximum inlet pressure. This allows for the hose-pressure drop (see the chart on p. 83), which is caused by friction as the air passes through the hose. To avoid this calculation, install a miniregulator at the gun to set the pressure.

Turn the fan-width and fluid-delivery valves clockwise so that they're closed. If your gun has a cheater valve (a built-in air regulator), make sure it's open. While the trigger is fully depressed, open the fluid-delivery valve a few turns, which regulates the amount of fluid going through the nozzle. Set it low for delicate spraying of edges and small areas, or open it up for spraying large surfaces. Spray a piece of scrapwood or some corrugated cardboard. Ideally, you want a fine and uniform pattern of droplets across the width of the spray. If you have coarse, large droplets, either the finish is too thin or the needle/nozzle is too large. The reverse is true if the gun sputters or spits. If the finish looks good, keep turning down the air pressure in 5-psi increments until you start to see the finish form a dimpled surface resembling an orange peel. Then raise the air back up 5 psi. Note this as the proper air pressure for the finish you're using. Operating the gun at the lowest pressure possible saves material by reducing bounce-back and overspray.

The fan-width control valve on the gun regulates the spray pattern. As you open the valve, the spray pattern becomes elongated (for more on spray patterns, see the sidebar at left). When you open the valve, you also may have to turn up the air pressure going into the gun, so it's a good idea to keep an eye on your regulator.

Setting up a turbine-driven gun Fully open the cheater valve on the gun. The correct air/liquid balance is established the same way as on a conversion gun. However, on most turbine guns, the position of the air cap determines the shape and orientation of the spray pattern. When the air cap's horns are in the horizontal position, the spray pattern is wide and oriented vertically. When you rotate the air cap 90 degrees, the spray pattern is horizontal. The intermediate position makes the spray pattern tight and round.

Mastering the Art of Spraying

Before spraying any piece of furniture, dismantle large items as much as you can. Remove backs from carcase pieces and remove drawer bottoms, if possible. If you have a complicated project that includes a lot of slats, consider finishing them before final assembly.

How much finish to apply Novice sprayers often get carried away with the ease of laying down a finish, so they apply too much at once.

You should aim for each coat to be about two thousandths of an inch thick, or in spraying terms, two mils. A mil gauge is a piece of metal with teeth in mil increments. To use the gauge, spray some finish onto an impermeable surface such as laminate or glass. Drag the gauge through the wet finish, keeping it 90 degrees to the surface and pressed down. Withdraw the gauge and note the first tooth that isn't coated with finish, as well as the one next to it that is coated. Your depth of finish will be an intermediate thickness between these marks. If you have trouble seeing clear finishes on the gauge, sprinkle talc on the wet teeth and blow it off. The talc will stick to the wet teeth.

The basic spray stroke Lay a flat board or a piece of cardboard on a pair of sawhorses to practice on. Hold the gun perpendicular to the surface, about 6 in. to 8 in. away and about 3 in. off the bottom left-hand corner. Depress the trigger until finish comes out, and move the gun across the board until you get 2 in. to 3 in. past the far edge. Do not arc your pass; rather, lock your forearm so that the gun moves across the board at a constant height and in a straight line. As you make another pass, overlap the first by 50 percent to 75 percent. Move the gun fast enough to avoid puddles of finish, but not so fast that the surface feels rough when it has dried.

I start with the surface closest to me and work toward the exhaust fan in my spray booth (see "Setting Up to Spray" on pp. 82–83) to reduce overspray landing on the wet finish and leaving it rough. Practice this basic "stroke" until it becomes second nature, because it is fundamental to all spraying.

Flat surfaces The basic spray technique for flat surfaces is called a crosshatch. Begin with the underside of the piece: At a 90 degree angle to the grain, start your first pass at the edge closest to you and spray a series of overlapping strokes. Then rotate the top 90 degrees (it helps to have it on a turntable) and spray with the grain.

Holding the still-dry edges, turn over the panel and place it back on the nail board. Spray the edges with the gun parallel to the surface, then bring the gun up to 45 degrees to the top and spray the edges again to get extra finish on them. Finally, repeat the cross-hatching on the top side.

If you get a drip, and you won't be damaging a delicate toner or glaze underneath, wipe the drip immediately with your finger and lightly respray the area.

Spraying Flat Surfaces

THE BASIC SPRAY STROKE

Hold the spray gun at the same distance from the workpiece for the entire pass over the surface. Start spraying off the edge of the workpiece and proceed over the surface. Stop spraying off the other edge.

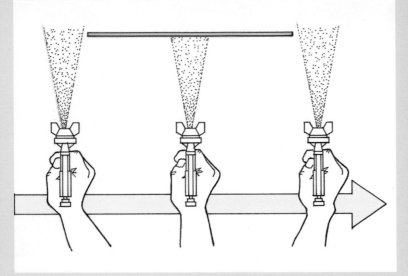

FINISH A PANEL IN FOUR STEPS

To achieve a good finish on a flat panel, you need even coverage on all surfaces. The use of a nail board and turntable allows you to finish the top surface while the bottom is still wet and to direct the spray (and the over-spray) toward an extractor fan.

SPRAY THE EDGES. With the gun parallel to the panel's surface, make one pass on all four edges.

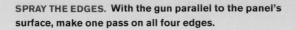

RECOAT THE EDGES. With the gun now at a 45° angle to the panel, give the edges a second coat of finish.

DEALING WITH RUNS. If you spot an area with too much finish, quickly wipe away the surplus and apply another light coat.

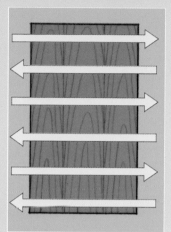

SPRAY ACROSS THE GRAIN.
Maintaining the gun at an
even height over the surface,
spray overlapping strokes
across the grain.

3

**THEN SPRAY WITH THE
GRAIN.** Turn the workpiece
90° and spray with the grain
in the second half of a
crosshatch pattern.

4

Spraying Furniture

CASE PIECES

GET DOWN, AND GET UNDER YOUR CABINET. Spray the underside of the shelves first (above). Then complete the inside of a cabinet by spraying the sides (right) followed by the tops of the shelves. In this way, the most noticeable surface is sprayed last and won't be affected by overspray.

AVOID RUNS ON VERTICAL SURFACES. Apply overlapping strokes from bottom to top, but do not apply a crosshatch spray across the grain, as too much finish likely will sag or run on a vertical surface.

Inside cabinets Spraying inside a cabinet is a lot easier if you remove the back. If you cannot remove the back, you'll get a face full of overspray unless you turn the air pressure way down, which may result in a poorly atomized finish. Start on the underside of the top and then the two sides, leaving the bottom last so that overspray doesn't settle there and create a rough finish. For each panel, spray all four edges first before doing the center. Rotate the piece so that you always spray toward the back of the booth; this way, the fan will draw the overspray away from the piece. Blow away the cloud of finish left inside by depressing the trigger of the gun slightly so that air but no finish comes through.

Verticals Start at the bottom and lay down a continuous layer of finish until you reach the top. Overlap each pass 50 percent—as though you were spraying a flat surface—but don't crosshatch, because the extra finish will cause runs. For face frames, adjust

RAISED PANELS

THE PROCEDURE IS IDENTICAL to that of a tabletop, with the addition of a first pass with the gun angled around the inside edge of the frame.

SLATS AND SPINDLES

WITH THE STOOL UPSIDE DOWN (above), spray the underside of the rails and the inside surfaces that are least visible. Flip the stool (left) and spray the visible areas, keeping the spray gun the same distance from the workpiece.

GRIDS

TREAT GRIDS AND FRAMES for glass-panel doors as a flat, continuous surface, and apply a crosshatch spray pattern.

the fan width to match the width of the frame members, if possible.

Complicated Pieces

To spray a stool or a chair, work from the less-visible parts to the most visible. With the piece upside down, spray the underside and inside areas. Though less visible, they still have to be finished. Turn over the stool and rest it on four screws driven into the feet to prevent the finish from pooling around the bottom of the legs.

Now spray the sides of the legs and the slats, working quickly to apply light coats. Finally, finish the outside surfaces that are most visible. As with vertical surfaces, the trick is to keep the coats of finish thin and to avoid sags and runs.

★ *Please note price estimates are from 2004.*

JEFF JEWITT restores furniture in Cleveland, Ohio, and is the author of *Taunton's Complete Illustrated Guide to Finishing* (2004).

Spray Finishing Done Right

BY ANDY CHARRON

GETTING A BLEMISH-FREE FINISH is easier than you think.

Quite a few woodworkers I know are unenthusiastic, even fearful, about spray finishing. They believe the equipment is too mysterious, too costly, and too hard to master. In fact, just the opposite is true. There are many simple-to-operate, reasonably priced spray systems out there. It took me less time to become proficient with a spray gun than it did to master a router. Best of all, the finish from a gun is often so smooth that I don't have to rub it out. Following sound spraying principles and knowing how to use the equipment helps me produce virtually flawless finishes.

Where to Spray

The best place to spray is in a booth where a powerful exhaust removes overspray and dust from the air. If you're spraying solvent-borne finishes, you really have no other choice than to use an explosion-proof spray booth. But they're costly. You don't need explosion-proof equipment to spray water-borne finishes, and they're getting better and better. You only need a place that is well-ventilated and clean. If you have the floor space, you can build a spray room that has an exhaust fan and intake filters to ensure a steady supply of clean, fresh air. No matter where you plan to spray, check with your local building officials first.

Careful Preparation Is Essential

How you prepare the surface is just as important as how you spray the finish. Sand the entire piece thoroughly (see the photo below right). For stained work, I usually raise the grain with a damp cloth, let the surface dry, and sand with 220 grit before I spray. For waterborne finishes and dyes, I sand to 180 grit and spray a light coat of dye stain or finish. This raises the grain and stiffens the fibers, making them easier to sand with 220 grit.

Spraying paint or pigmented lacquers is more involved. Opaque finishes highlight tiny imperfections. They often require at least two rounds of filling, sanding, and priming before the wood is ready to be sprayed.

Thin the Finish to a Sprayable Consistency

Life would be easier if you could always pour finish straight from the can into a spray pot and begin applying it. But occasionally, you'll have to thin it. Which thinner you use and how much you add will depend on the material you're applying, the spray system you're using, and what the piece will be used for. Some manufacturers do a lousy job of providing thinning information. If the appropriate thinner is listed on the label, use it. Because some cans of finish say that the contents don't need to be thinned, they don't list a thinner. If this is the case, you generally can thin the finish with the solvent that's recommended for cleanup.

Finding the correct viscosity The viscosity of a finish is a measurement of its resistance to flow. Thinning a finish lowers the viscosity, which allows it to be broken into smaller particles (or atomized) more easily by the spray gun. The finer the atomization, the smoother the appearance.

Thinners can eliminate common spray problems (see the sidebar on pp. 96–97) like orange peel, but if used improperly, thinners actually cause problems. Waterborne finishes are especially sensitive to thinning. Over-thinning can prevent the finish from forming a clear, hard film.

Some spray-gun manufacturers recommend finish viscosity for a particular

SPRAYED FINISHES ARE ONLY AS GOOD as the surface below. The author primed this bookcase and now sands it with 220-grit paper in preparation for spraying on a tinted waterborne lacquer top coat.

SPRAYING TAKES A BIT OF PRACTICE. Surface preparation, finish consistency, and technique all are important.

needle/tip combination. This information may be given as a ratio or a percentage of thinner and finish. The viscosity also may be given as the number of seconds it takes to empty a certain size viscosity cup. Viscosity cups have small holes in the bottom, which let liquid drain through (see the photo on p. 94). Appropriately sized cups are available from most spray-system makers.

Room conditions are a factor Temperature and humidity dramatically affect how much thinner to use in a finish and how it will spray. Low temperature and high humidity are not especially conducive to spraying. Even if you follow all the labels exactly, you may have to adjust the amount of thinner you add. You can keep records of how much thinner you need for different conditions. After a while, you'll get a feel for this.

Straining the Finish and Filling the Pot

Your finish and your equipment should be as clean as possible because a speck of dirt or dried finish could ruin the job. To remove impurities, pour the finish through a strainer or filter (available at paint-supply dealers). As an added precaution, you can install a filter on the end of the dip tube that draws finish from the pot, or put an in-line filter near the gun. To keep the air that comes from the compressor dry and clean, I run the line through a canister-type separator, which filters out water, oil, and dirt before they get in the hose supplying air to the gun.

Selecting Suitable Fluid Tips and Air Caps

The fluid tip in a spray gun controls the amount of finish that gets deposited on a surface. In general, lighter finishes require a small tip. Thicker materials (or those with a higher percentage of solids) require larger

Spray the Least Visible Areas First

Before spraying, make a dry run through the whole process. To help prevent you from overcoating or missing areas, visualize and then practice the sequence of spray strokes. Although the order in which you spray parts of a piece may vary slightly, there are a few rules of thumb worth following: Start with the least visible areas, such as drawer bottoms and cabinet backs, and work your way to those parts that will be seen. For example, spray the edges of tabletops, doors, and shelves before the tops. This minimizes the overspray on the most visible surfaces. Working from the inside out holds true for case pieces, too, as shown in the series of photos at right. Always work from the wettest edge, so you can easily blend areas you've just sprayed. Where possible, move the gun away from your body, toward the exhaust fan (assuming you have one). This will help prevent overspray from settling on previously sprayed areas, and it will give you an unclouded view, too.

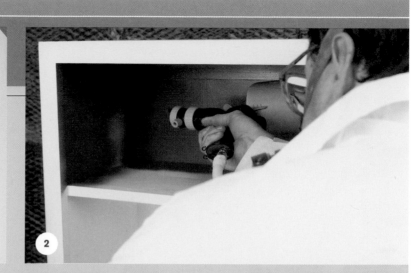

SPRAY OVERHEAD CORNERS, and then fill in the inside top.

COAT INTERIOR BACK AND SIDES. These areas won't be highly visible when the piece is finished.

SHELF TOPS AND FRONTS. Remember to overlap strokes.

FINISH THE FACE FRAME. Begin with the inside edges, and then move to the front of the case.

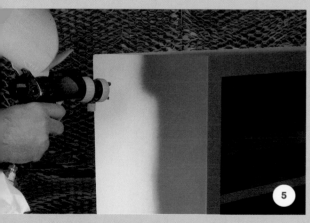

DO THE EXTERIOR CABINET SIDES and front corners.

SPRAY THE TOP. By leaving the top for last, the most visible part of the case isn't marred by overspray.

**CHECK THE FINISH WITH A VIS-
COSITY CUP. A stopwatch and
the recommended viscosity cup
show whether thinner must be
added. Once thinned, the finish
is passed through a filter.**

be done by changing air caps. If you are
using a waterborne finish with a turbine
and a bleeder-type (constant air flow) gun,
make sure that the nozzle stays clean. These
guns are prone to blobs of finish drying on
the air cap and then blemishing the work.

Adjusting the Gun

Spray guns come with adjustments for air
and fluid. The type of finish being sprayed,
the size of the object to be coated, and the
speed of application all play a role in deciding how to control the fluid and air. I
always test my fan pattern and finish delivery rate on scrap wood or cardboard so that
I can make adjustments before I actually
spray the piece.

Turbine-driven HVLP systems Adjusting
a turbine-powered spray gun is a simple
process: No matter what type of gun you
own, the idea is to start air flowing through
the gun first, and then introduce finish
slowly until it flows continuously and evenly.
The gun should apply a full, wet coat with
no heavy spots or misses. From this point,
you can open or close either knob to
obtain the best spray rate and fan pattern.

If you want to spray a lot of material in
a hurry, open the fluid control more. If you
are coating large surfaces, widen the fan
pattern. If you're trying to achieve a fine
finish or you're spraying small items, you'll
have more control of how much finish is
applied and where it lands by restricting the
fan and fluid. But remember, how you set
one knob affects the other. For example, if
you increase the air flow without adjusting
the fluid, the finish may be too fine. Con-
versely, opening the fluid control without
widening the fan can cause runs and sags.
At the ideal settings, the finish will coat
evenly and flow together well.

Compressor-driven systems With high-
pressure spray guns and conversion-air
HVLP guns (both powered by a compressor),

fluid tips. The air cap in a spray gun controls the velocity of the air, which governs
how finely the fluid is atomized. Air caps
with smaller holes cause the air to leave
the gun at a higher velocity, thus producing
finer atomization. Air caps are matched with
fluid tips to give optimum performance.

Most guns come equipped with a standard setup appropriate for several finishes.
The setup includes a fluid tip that's about
.050 in. dia. and a corresponding air cap.
The standard setup will produce acceptable
results with most finishes, but sometimes it's
worth trying other combinations of fluid
tips and air caps.

In a turbine-driven HVLP system, the
amount of air feeding the gun is constant,
so adjustments to the air pressure can only

TURNTABLE FOR EVEN, QUICK COATS. After arranging trophy bases on a lazy Susan, the author sprays with an HVLP gun.

PLAN FOR DRYING. The author uses racks to cure his spray-finished items. The area is warm, dry, and dust-free.

you have the ability to control the air pressure entering the gun in addition to adjusting the fluid rate and fan shape. Getting all three adjustments coordinated can be a bit tricky and takes some trial and error, but being able to regulate the air pressure at the gun allows more spraying options.

Develop a Spray Strategy

Regardless of the size and shape of the object you're spraying, the main thing to keep in mind is that you want to spray an even coat over the entire piece. Always spray the finish in several thin coats rather than one heavy one. Lighter coats are less likely to run, dry faster, and make sanding between coats easier.

If the pieces you are spraying are so small that the air from the gun blows them all over the place, try placing them on a piece of screen or wire mesh. I prefer spraying small parts with my turbine HVLP gun because the spray is softer. A good production tip for spraying many small pieces is to put them on a lazy Susan and spray several at once (see the photo above left). Rotate

the turntable as you spray so you don't build up too heavy a coat on the pieces.

Position large work on sawhorses or a stand so that the height is comfortable. You shouldn't have to bend, reach, or otherwise contort your arm or body while you're spraying. You should be able to turn and move the work easily. I sometimes support the work on stickers or points (blunted drywall screws work well) to make sure that the bottom edge gets good coverage.

Spraying Uniformly

To maintain even spray coverage, there are a few things to remember. Grip the gun firmly, but not so tightly that your hand gets tired or uncomfortable. Point the nose of the gun so it's perpendicular to the worksurface, and hold the gun at the same distance from the work on each pass. Move the gun parallel to surfaces, not in an arcing, sweeping motion. Begin your stroke 6 in. or so before the gun is over the wood, and continue the same distance beyond the other side. Trigger the gun a split second after you start your motion, and keep spraying until

Correcting Spray-Finish Troubles

Fine Woodworking magazine's consulting editor Chris Minick found big improvements in his finishes when he switched to spray equipment. But the transition wasn't painless. Here's his list of common spray problems and, where they're not obvious, the solutions.

ORANGE PEEL

COTTONING OR BLUSH

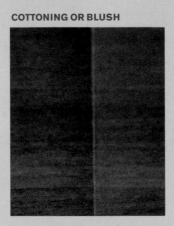

WHITE SPOTS

SAGS AND RUNS

1. Atomization pressure too low: Increase pressure and adjust fluid.	(Right half shows blush) 1. High humidity: Dehumidify shop, or add retarder to finish.	1. Water contamination in spray equipment: Install water separator in air line.	1. Coat too heavy: Decrease fluid flow to spray gun.
2. Spray gun too far from work: Maintain 6-in. to 10-in. gun distance.	2. Improper thinner: Use only recommended thinner.	2. Water on work surface: Dry work surface before spraying.	2. Spray gun too close to surface: Maintain 6-in. to 10-in. gun distance.
3. Coating viscosity too high: Thin to correct application viscosity.	3. Moisture in spray equipment: Install water separator in air line.		3. Thinning solvent drying too slowly: Use faster evaporating thinner.
4. Not enough coating thickness for proper flow.			4. Drafty spray room.

your arm stops. As you spray across the piece, move your arm steadily and smoothly without changing speed.

For most HVLP guns, hold the gun about 6 in. to 8 in. from the surface. This will let you spray a full, wet coat with minimal overspray and decent coverage. Move the gun at about the same speed you would a brush. Each pass should overlap the previous one by about half. When spraying small objects or tight places, reduce the flow and move the gun closer. To avoid clouds of overspray and bounce-back, work from inside corners out. Use more wrist action, and trigger more quickly. On large areas, increase the flow, pull the gun back an inch or two, and make passes in opposite directions. I lightly spray across the grain to make a tack coat. Then I immediately spray with the grain.

In situations where your spray passes intersect, such as the stretcher-to-leg joint of a chair, release the trigger a bit sooner than you normally would. This will feather out the finish. If overlapping passes still give you a problem, mask off adjacent areas.

AT EDGE

Corner profile too sharp:
Slightly radius 90° edges.
Drafts on one side of
workpiece.
One side of workpiece
warmer than other.

CRATERING

(Solid chunk In center)
1. Solid contaminant (usually
from nonloading sandpaper)
lowers surface tension: Sand
defect, and wipe entire surface with mineral spirits.

FISHEYES

1. Silicone or wax residue from
paint stripper or old finish:
Wipe surface with mineral
spirits; mist coats (let each
dry) to trap contaminants.
2. Oil in spray equipment (usually from compressor): Install
oil separator in air line.

MICROBUBBLES

(Haze, waterborne finish only)
1. Coating is drying too fast:
Add retarder to finish.
2. Defoamer deactivates in
waterborne finish: Don't use
waterborne finish that's more
than 1 year old.
3. Atomization pressure
too high.

Drying and Cleaning Up are Critical

It's easy to forget that once you spray a piece, the finish needs a warm, dry, and dust-free place to cure. If you don't have a separate drying area (see the top right photo on p. 95), production in your shop can grind to a halt. Even if you have a designated area, storing a number of wet cabinets, doors, drawers, and trim pieces can be a problem. I use a system of racks to dry components and store them for short periods. Plywood trays, slipped into old baker's racks, come in handy when I have to dry lots of small pieces. When I'm drying round or odd-shaped items, like balusters, I hang them on an overhead wire from swivel hooks. Each piece can be rotated and sprayed and then hung in my drying area.

I have made it a ritual to clean my spray gun thoroughly while my work is drying. After cleaning the parts with the solvent recommended on the finish container, I dry them with compressed air. Then I coat all the fluid passages with alcohol and let it evaporate before I store the gun in its case.

ANDY CHARRON runs Charron Wood Products in Windsor, Vermont.

All About Thinning Finishes

BY JEFF JEWITT

It's a rare woodworker who is not intimidated by the cans of solvents lining the shelves in a hardware store. The multisyllabic names are reminders of less-than-productive school chemistry classes, while the dire health warnings are equally off-putting. The temptation is to grab something vaguely familiar, hope that it is compatible with the finish you are using, and leave as fast as possible.

But it need not be like this. I will guide you through the world of solvents—the good, the bad, and the unpronounceable. I will show you which solvents are appropriate for water- or oil-based finishes, shellacs, or solvent lacquers, whether you are spraying, brushing, or wiping on the finish.

A Very Quick Word About Chemistry

Almost all finishing materials contain liquids that are volatile, meaning they evaporate during the drying and curing of the finish. These liquids, called solvents and thinners, make the finishing material less viscous for easier application.

Chemists distinguish between solvents and thinners: Solvents dissolve or break up finishing resins and reduce viscosity, while thinners merely reduce the viscosity. Dis-

solving shellac flakes with denatured alcohol is the only occasion a woodworker is likely to use a solvent as such. For this chapter, I use the terms *solvent* and *thinner* interchangeably, as many woodworkers do.

I have divided finishes into four families, roughly in order of the toxicity of their solvents: water-based, shellac, oil-based, and solvent-based lacquer. For each family, I cover the range of compatible thinners and the points to consider when choosing one.

Thinning Water-Based Finishes Takes More Than Water

The widespread use of water-based finishes is rather new, and in many cases the chemistry behind it is still being fine-tuned. Many woodworkers are aware of water-based versions of lacquer and polyurethane, but water-based varieties of varnish, gel stain, and Danish-oil finishes are also available. While the novice might assume they would be the easiest finishes to thin because they are made up mostly of water, their chemical complexity makes them the least-forgiving finishes to tamper with.

You can get into serious problems if you add too much water. Usually 5 percent to 10 percent is fine for viscosity adjustments

How Much Time Do You Need?

O ne of the reasons for adding solvents is to control the rate at which the finish dries. This control is desirable for any method of application. When spraying a vertical surface, too slow a drying time may cause the finish to run, while a finish that evaporates too fast may leave an orange-peel appearance. When brushing, the right solvent can maintain a wet edge yet not attract dust by taking forever to dry. In the charts, the drying time of a solvent is rated as slow if it acts as a retarder (slows down the drying time). A rating of medium means that the solvent doesn't significantly change the drying properties of a finish, although the drying time of any thinned finish will speed up somewhat. And fast solvents do just that: speed up the drying time. The actual speed will vary based on application methods and environmental conditions.

THE SLOW AND THE FAST. Mineral spirits and naphtha were simultaneously brushed onto a board. Three minutes later, the naphtha had almost evaporated, while the mineral spirits was still wet.

Water-based Finishes

Among the finishing families, the evaporation rate of water-based finishes is the most difficult to adjust. They typically require a specific retarder, while plain water should only be added sparingly.

Thinner	Drying Time	Comments
Retarder (water, glycol ether and additives)	Medium	Used to combat lap marks when brushing or orange peel when spraying. Follow the advice of the finish manufacturer carefully and use only the recommended retarder; otherwise, the chemical balance may be upset, rendering the product useless.
Water	Fast	To avoid upsetting the chemical balance, never add more than 10% water. If the product is too thick to atomize properly for spraying or if it streaks when brushing or wiping, thinning may be required. If the humidity is 90% or more, don't add water because it will act as a retarder and lead to excessive drying time.

A BRUSHED FINISH should go down without leaving lap marks. If you have trouble keeping a wet edge because the finish dries too quickly, which may happen in warm, dry weather, add a small amount of retarder to a water-based finish.

(to make it spray or brush better), but more than that can disrupt the chemical makeup of the finish, which will have a negative effect on how the finish forms a film.

For a finish that dries too fast, a better alternative is to use a retarder. A retarder is typically used in hot, dry conditions. It helps you avoid orange peel by giving the finish more time to flow out and achieve a level surface. Be sure to use a retarder recommended by the finish manufacturer. The wrong retarder can upset the chemical balance of the finish.

When spraying a water-based finish, before adding water or a retarder, try to compensate for viscosity by changing to a larger needle/nozzle and making adjustments to your finishing environment or technique. Spray thinner coats when it's hot and humid, and arrange fans so that air blows gently across the finish as it dries.

Shellac Is Compatible With More Than Alcohol

Shellac is one of the oldest finishes in woodworking. No other finish can match the depth and clarity it brings to wood, but its lack of durability makes it unsuitable for surfaces subject to heavy use.

Shellac is available in dried flakes that are dissolved in alcohol or in ready-to-use liquid form. For both premixed shellac and shellac flakes, the best all-around thinner is denatured alcohol.

Shellac

Most woodworkers use only denatured alcohol to thin shellac, but several other solvents offer slower evaporation rates for brushing shellac or spraying it on a hot and dry day.

Thinner	Drying Time	Comments
Pure gum spirit turpentine	Slow	For an effective retarder, add a teaspoon to about 4 oz. of liquid shellac.
Isobutanol	Medium/slow	Acts as a retarder but is difficult to find and has a very strong odor.
Isopropanol	Medium/slow	A suitable retarder when brushing shellac. Auto-parts stores sell it as gas-line antifreeze. Check the label to make sure that isopropanol is the only component. An alternative source for 99% pure isopropanol is www.chemistrystore.com.
Denatured alcohol	Medium/fast	Will slightly speed up drying time and improve the flow and atomization of heavy (3-lb. cut) shellac. It is the main solvent and thinner for shellac. Specific-brand formulas with different additives are available.
Methanol	Very fast	Although no longer available to the consumer market, professional finishers can still obtain the product. Speeds up drying times considerably.

As shellac is sprayed, the solvents evaporate, cooling the surface of the workpiece. If the temperature falls below the dew point, moisture condenses on the surface, causing a cloudy appearance in the finish known as blushing. If you are spraying shellac in hot, humid weather, you need to slow down the drying rate to avoid blushing. Suitable retarders include butanol or isopropanol, the latter being found at auto-parts stores as a gas-line antifreeze. Do not use rubbing alcohol; even though the active ingredient is isopropanol, the other 30 percent to 50 percent is water, which will not improve your finish. Glycol ether such as lacquer retarder also slows the drying time of shellac, but the finish may remain soft and be more easily damaged.

A retarder is also useful when you are brushing shellac on a large surface, such as a tabletop. If the shellac dries too quickly, you risk applying the finish to an area adjacent to one where the finish has already started to set up, preventing the edges of the brush strokes from blending together. Adding a teaspoon of pure gum spirit turpentine to approximately 4 oz. of liquid shellac acts as a retarder. With a retarder added, the first line of finish will remain wet until the second line can be brushed on and the two can blend together.

MORE BRUSHING, LESS RUSH-ING. The addition of turpentine slows the drying time of shellac, allowing you to keep a wet edge while brushing a large surface. You can even go back and tip off the surface.

Oil-Based Finishes

The petroleum industry has produced a large range of solvents compatible with oil-based finishes. These range from slow-evaporating kerosene to fast-evaporating ketone.

Thinner	Drying Time	Comments
Kerosene	Slow	Used in small amounts, kerosene is very effective as a retarder when brushing on an oil finish in dry weather.
Odorless mineral spirits	Slow	Mineral spirits becomes odorless mineral spirits by removing the aromatics. This product is commonly available at art-supply stores as well as hardware stores. Acts as a retarder.
Mineral spirits/paint thinner	Medium	Use to change the viscosity without impacting the drying time significantly. Good for adding to a finish that will be brushed. Can also be used to thin gel varnishes that dry too fast and streak.
Pure gum spirit turpentine	Medium	No longer used much in commercial finishing due to the variable quality. The rosin content is not reported on the can, but a batch with high rosin may leave a soft finish. The high price relative to paint thinner is another drawback.
Xylene	Medium/fast	Best used for thinning conversion varnishes.
VM&P naphtha	Fast	Varnish maker's and painter's naphtha is the best solvent for fast evaporation. Use it when spraying in cold weather, on vertical surfaces, or when using varnish or polyurethane as a wipe-on finish.
Toluene	Fast	Dries slightly faster than VM&P naphtha but has a very strong odor. For consumers, naphtha is a better choice.
Acetone (ketone)	Fast	Add to a thick varnish when spraying a single, heavy coat to avoid runs and sags. When applied over a previous coat, may cause wrinkling of the finish.

Hydrocarbon Solvents and Oil-Based Finishes Offer the Most Choices

Linseed, tung, and Danish oils, oil-based varnishes and polyurethanes, oil paint, and waxes make up the largest family of finishes and are the products most woodworkers think of when it comes to finishing. These finishes are thinned with two groups of solvents: hydrocarbons and terpenes.

Hydrocarbons (kerosene, mineral spirits, naphtha, paint thinner, toluene, xylene) are derived from petroleum oil.

Terpenes (turpentine, d-limonene) are derived from plants, with turpentine coming from pine trees and d-limonene from citrus trees. These two solvents are nearly always interchangeable with hydrocarbons. D-limonene has a pretty distinctive citrus smell that makes it more pleasant to work with, but it's hard to find. Its toxicity and flammability are about equal to mineral spirits, but the evaporation rate is slower.

Because of the high cost of extracting turpentine, this classic thinner has all but been replaced with mineral spirits. A drawback to using turpentine is the rosin content, which can vary depending on what trees were processed in each particular batch. If the rosin content is high in the can you are using, the finish will remain soft; however, you will not find a measurement on the side of the can.

The two best thinners to use are mineral spirits and naphtha. Mineral spirits is best for maintaining a wet edge when brushing, while naphtha is better for spraying or wiping. Kerosene can be added in very small amounts (6 to 12 drops per pint) to oil-based stains to slow them down for easier application on large surfaces.

The Right Retarder Makes Lacquers Easier to Use

Solvent-based lacquer finishes have traditionally been the mainstays of commercial furniture makers and professional finishers. They are not as popular with hobbyists because of their reputation for needing expensive spraying facilities.

Solvent-based lacquer is thinned with lacquer thinner, a blend of ketones, alcohol, and hydrocarbons. By adjusting the ratio of these components, manufacturers can tailor a thinner to be fast, medium, or slow evaporating. Most woodworking finish suppliers

TO THIN OR NOT TO THIN. Some finishes, particularly oil-based ones, come with a warning not to thin the contents. In finishes advertised as having a "clean-air formula," any addition of solvent would place the finish above the emissions limit agreed upon with the government.

Lacquer

Besides the generic medium-speed lacquer thinner, slow and fast formulations are also available. The evaporation of lacquer can be slowed by adding a retarder or accelerated by adding acetone.

Thinner	Drying Time	Comments
Lacquer retarder	Slow	It's best not to mix retarder directly with a brushing lacquer. Instead, add 1 oz. to 2 oz. of retarder to 1 qt. standard (medium) lacquer thinner, then add small amounts of the mix to a finish.
Slow lacquer thinner	Medium/slow	Most lacquer thinner available in hardware or woodworking stores has a medium-speed evaporation rate. The best place to find slow- or fast-evaporating lacquer thinner is at an auto-finishing supply store. If in doubt about their suitability, an alternative is to add lacquer retarder to a medium-speed thinner. This will produce a slow-evaporating thinner needed on hot days to avoid blushing and when spraying a horizontal surface to improve flow-out. Fast-evaporating thinner is recommended for cool weather and when spraying vertical surfaces. This can be made by adding acetone to a medium-speed lacquer thinner.
Medium lacquer thinner	Medium	
Fast lacquer thinner	Fast	
Acetone	Very fast	Acetone evaporates so fast that it is prone to leave a finish blushed unless the humidity is very low. Woodworkers in Arizona spraying during the summer may get away with using it.

stock only medium-speed thinner. The best place to find fast- and slow-evaporating lacquer thinners is an auto-finishing store. Fast-evaporating thinner prevents sagging on vertical surfaces, but if you can't find it, use acetone. Unless you are spraying in very low humidity, however, an acetone-thinned finish is susceptible to blushing because of its very fast evaporation rate.

Slow-evaporating thinners allow the finish to flow out and level better on horizontal surfaces. For this reason, slow-evaporating thinner is sometimes called "warm weather" thinner. An alternative to slow-evaporating thinner is to add lacquer retarder (glycol ether) to a standard lacquer thinner, then add the mix to a finish.

Sources

Mapa Glove
www.mapaglove.com

Material Safety Data Sheet (MSDS)
http://siri.uvm/msds

National Institute for Occupational Safety and Health (NIOSH)
www.cdc.gov/niosh

ADJUST YOUR LACQUER FOR EVERY OCCASION. When spraying a vertical surface, it is important that the finish dries before it has a chance to sag and run.

SEE HOW IT RUNS. The top bar of black lacquer had fast-evaporating acetone added. The lower bar was thinned with slow-evaporating lacquer thinner, giving the finish time to run before it could dry.

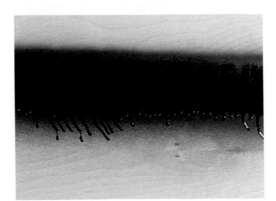

For more information on the dangers of a particular solvent, and to find out what type of respirator to use, check its material safety data sheet (MSDS) available online and National Institute for Occupational Safety and Health (NIOSH) (see "Sources" for both).

JEFF JEWITT restores furniture in Cleveland, Ohio, and is the author of *Taunton's Complete Illustrated Guide to Finishing* (2004).

The Right Glove for Each Solvent

When using solvents, many wood-workers protect their hands with disposable latex or vinyl gloves. Inevitably a particular solvent seems to eat through the glove as if it wasn't there, resulting in chapped skin or even chemical burns.

Shown here are disposable and reusable gloves made of latex, nitrile, vinyl, and neoprene. Less important than what the glove is made of is to remember that disposable gloves should be used only for splash protection, such as when blending a finish or brushing one on. For more sustained contact, such as when using a solvent to clean a spray gun or wiping on a finish, use heavy-duty gloves. Unfortunately, no one glove is suitable for all solvents.

Specific information on how different glove materials stand up to various solvents can be found at Mapa® Glove's website (see "Sources") as well as other manufacturers' sites.

LATEX
Used primarily for mixing dye powders and applying water-based dyes. The main advantage of disposable latex gloves is their flexibility and feel, which make them good for doing detailed work. Neither type of glove shown will stand up to oils or hydrocarbon derivatives (mineral spirits, naphtha, paint thinner, or kerosene).

NITRILE
Nitrile gloves offer protection from almost any solvent a woodworker is likely to use. The only exception is a solvent that contains a ketone such as acetone. The disposable version offers more protection than the other two types of disposable gloves, but they are harder to find and are more expensive.

VINYL
OK for powdered dyes and dyes in a water solution. Disposable vinyl gloves are the cheapest protection available, but they tear more easily than disposable latex ones. Avoid contact with ketones and aromatic solvents. The thicker gloves offer good protection but at the expense of a clumsy feel.

NEOPRENE
This is another excellent choice for regular contact with most solvents, except lacquer thinner, where nitrile is a better choice.

Aerosol Finishes

BY CHRIS A. MINICK

No doubt about it; I am a confirmed finishing junkie. My finishing arsenal consists of a bevy of expensive brushes, half a dozen spray guns, and more cans of finish than I care to count. It may seem odd, given my well-stocked shop, that my weapon of choice for finishing small projects is usually the common and much maligned aerosol spray can.

Aerosol finishes aren't what they used to be. Gone are the days of sputtering low-tech paints. They've been replaced with professional-quality wood finishes in an amazingly broad array of types. A trip to your local home center will reveal spray cans of varnish, lacquer, stains, toners, water-based finishes, and even precatalyzed finishes.

What about durability? It doesn't seem logical that an easy-to-use finish should yield good performance results. To satisfy my curiosity, I started a long-term test a few years ago comparing aerosol lacquer and varnish with their brush-on cousins. The test results are impressive: I found that most of the aerosol finishes have essentially the same stain, scratch, and solvent resistance as the brush-on variety, if applied in a thick-enough finish.

Before learning the few tricks that make finishing with aerosols effective and easy, it is best to start by learning how they operate.

Choosing an Aerosol Finish

A CHOICE OF FINISHES. Finishes available in aerosol cans include polyurethane, lacquer, water-based polyurethane, shellac, and spar varnish.

Finish Type	Sample Brands	Advantages	Disadvantages
Acrylic lacquer	Sherwin-Williams® Krylon ALLPRO® Spray Clear Acrylic Water Master® Clear Acrylic	• Fast dry time • Clear film	• Pinholes are possible during hot weather
Nitrocellulose lacquer	Deft® Behlen Rust-Oleum®	• Available as gloss, satin, or flat • Easy to sand	• Medium dry time • Heavy solvent odor
Oil-based	Zar® polyurethane Minwax spar urethane	• Good leveling qualities	• Slow dry time • Difficult to sand • Hard to repair
Water-based	Minwax® Polycrylic Behr® polyurethane	• Little solvent odor • Nonyellowing cast	• Bluish tint on dark wood • Raises grain on first coat • Slow dry time in humid weather
Shellac	Zinsser® Bulls Eye®	• Fast dry time • Good adhesion on oily woods • Natural color • Easy to sand	• Produces "fat edge" when applied in heavy coat

A Diluted Solution Is What Makes Aerosols Work

When the spray-can nozzle (known as the actuator in spray-can lingo) is pushed down, a small valve opens, allowing the head pressure in the can to force a mixture of finish resin, solvent, and propellant up the dip tube and out of the nozzle. As the finish solution leaves the tip, a liquefied propellant instantly vaporizes, exploding the finish and solvent mixture into millions of droplets.

Because the dip tube and actuator orifice of a typical aerosol can are rather small compared with the similar parts of a spray gun, the liquid finish in the can must be very thin to spray properly. Consequently, most aerosol finishes contain less than half the solids and significantly more solvent than the same volume of their nonaerosol cousins. A ratio of high solvent to low solids is a recipe for runs, drips, and sags if ever I heard one. These problems are easily avoided, though.

Nozzle design makes the difference

Aerosol cans are not all created equal, especially when it comes to nozzle design. Some aerosols spray an evenly shaped tapered fan pattern similar to the best conventional spray guns, while basic aerosol nozzles produce a simple doughnut-shaped cone pattern. In my experience, aerosol nozzles that fan out the finish are easier to control and provide fewer runs than those that spray conical patterns (see the photos and drawings on the facing page).

When shopping for an aerosol finish, remove the cap and inspect the nozzle. Fan nozzles will be made from two pieces of plastic: a large button actuator with a small plastic disc inserted in the face. This easy-to-spot disc has a raised line running across the orifice. The disc can be rotated to produce either a vertical or horizontal fan, a handy feature when spraying large projects. Cone spray actuators, on the other hand, can be made from one or two pieces of plastic but have no line. While you are at the store, pick up a plastic trigger handle (see the bottom photos on p. 112). This handle dramatically improves control and reduces finger fatigue, turning a simple spray can into a functioning spray gun.

You Can't Cover Up Poor Preparation

Someone much wiser than me once said, "Cleanliness is next to godliness." I can't vouch for that, but I do know that cleanliness is a very important part of finishing, especially when you're using aerosol cans. Heavy-bodied brush-on finishes are more forgiving when it comes to dirt or grime:

SPRAY GUN VS. SPRAY CAN. **The left half of the panel received two coats of lacquer from a spray gun. The right half received two coats of lacquer from an aerosol can. The aerosol finish is only half as thick as the spray-gun finish.**

They tend to bridge over the offending contamination, whereas thin aerosol finishes often pull away from it.

Dust creates an uneven stippled look in the dry finish while oily or waxy residue results in a moon-cratered appearance on the dried surface. Make sure all surfaces to be finished are free of dirt and grease before you start because fixing the problem after the fact means sanding off the entire finish and starting over. Before starting the finishing ritual, I make it a habit to vacuum the sanding dust thoroughly from my projects, as opposed to wiping with a tack rag, which just moves around the dust.

Proper Technique Yields a Flawless Finish

The method for spraying with an aerosol can is quickly learned, but as with any new finishing technique or product, practice on some scrap until you are comfortable. Shake the can vigorously up and down for a minute or until any agitator balls inside are loose (these are not present in most clear finishes), then swirl the can for one minute to blend the ingredients. It is good practice to swirl the can occasionally during the finishing job to ensure that the ingredients stay well mixed.

I get better results if I start the spray pattern from the front portion of the project and work toward the back, but feel free to experiment. The distance you hold the can from the surface is a function of the spray-nozzle geometry, the amount and type of propellant in the can, and the viscosity of the liquid, but in general the distance is anywhere from 6 in. to 12 in. Follow the manufacturer's recommendations on the side of the can. Trigger the aerosol can 2 in. to 3 in. off the edge of the piece and continue in one smooth motion across the entire width, finally releasing the trigger 2 in. to 3 in. past the other edge (see the drawings at right). This method eliminates puddling at the beginning and end of the stroke. Spray in short bursts, stopping at the end of each stroke. Repeat the procedure, overlapping each successive swath about 50 percent until the entire surface is covered.

Turn the piece 90 degrees and spray another light coat (called boxing in spray-finishing lingo). Avoid heavy coats. It is easier to spray on another coat than it is to sand out a run. Let the finish dry, then repeat the entire process until you are satisfied with the appearance.

The number of coats for maximum protection varies with the percentage of solids in the individual finish. As a crude rule of thumb, for decorative projects I apply multiple coats until the pores on tight-grained wood are filled with finish. Projects that will see heavy use get two or three additional coats after that. In general, I use satin finishes because they hide defects that a gloss finish would highlight.

The technique for rubbing out an aerosol finish can be identical to that for any other kind of finish. However, because each coat of finish is so thin, it is possible to sand out any defects such as dust specks, apply a final show coat, and buff that with a dry rag to give a silky smooth finish.

Always clear the nozzle after use by turning the can upside down and spraying

A Choice of Nozzles

Aerosol cans are equipped with one of two nozzle designs. The basic model sprays a cone-shaped pattern. A better design sprays an evenly shaped tapered fan pattern similar to that made by conventional spray guns.

BASIC
This nozzle's conical spray pattern makes it difficult to spray an even coat

BETTER
This style of nozzle produces an adjustable fan-shaped spray pattern.

Cans with a horizontal fan nozzle produce a long, elliptical spray pattern.

A FAN OF THIS CAN. The raised lines on both sides of the pinhole indicate that the nozzle can be rotated 90° to shift the spray pattern.

ADJUSTING THE ORIENTATION. A pair of pliers may be used to turn the nozzle to get a vertical spray pattern.

With the nozzle rotated, the spray pattern becomes vertical, which makes it easier to get into back corners of projects.

on some scrap until nothing but propellant is coming from the nozzle. In this way, the actuator won't be clogged with dried finish the next time you try to use it.

Don't Spray When It's Hot and Humid

Most aerosol finishes perform best at temperatures around 75°F and low relative humidity, conditions rarely seen in most woodshops. With a conventional spray finish, the solvent can be manipulated to suit various atmospheric conditions, but because aerosol finishes come in a sealed pressurized can, you cannot adjust the solvent mixture to account for less-than-ideal conditions.

This means that some finishes will almost certainly blush when sprayed on a hot, humid day. Blush occurs when the rapid evaporation of the solvent from a finish cools the surface to below the dew point of the surrounding hot, humid air. Water vapor in the air then condenses into liquid water on the surface of this cool finish. This in turn forces some of the finish resin to crystallize into microscopic white specks of solid

Applying an Aerosol Finish

SHAKEN, THEN STIRRED. Before being used, all aerosol cans should be shaken up and down (far left) to dislodge any solids that have settled, and then swirled around (left) to combine the solids with the propellant and the solvent.

INSTANT SPRAY GUN. An accessory handle makes spraying any aerosol much easier and more precise.

finish. Avoiding blush is fairly easy: Don't finish when both the temperature and the humidity are high.

If you do end up with blush on your project, all is not lost. It can usually be eliminated by waiting for the humidity to go down and then spritzing a light coat of the same finish over the entire project. The solvents in the fresh coat often will release the trapped moisture in the dried finish, eliminating the blush. You also can minimize the chances of blush if you can match your finish to the weather conditions. I've found through trial and error that aerosol acrylic lacquer finishes have fewer tendencies to blush than aerosol nitrocellulose lacquer finishes when it is hot and humid, while aerosol varnishes are virtually blush-proof any time of year.

Aerosol Cans Require Respect

Without a doubt, the ready-to-use, spray-it-and-forget-it nature of aerosol finishes makes them a valuable asset in any shop; however, this convenience comes with a

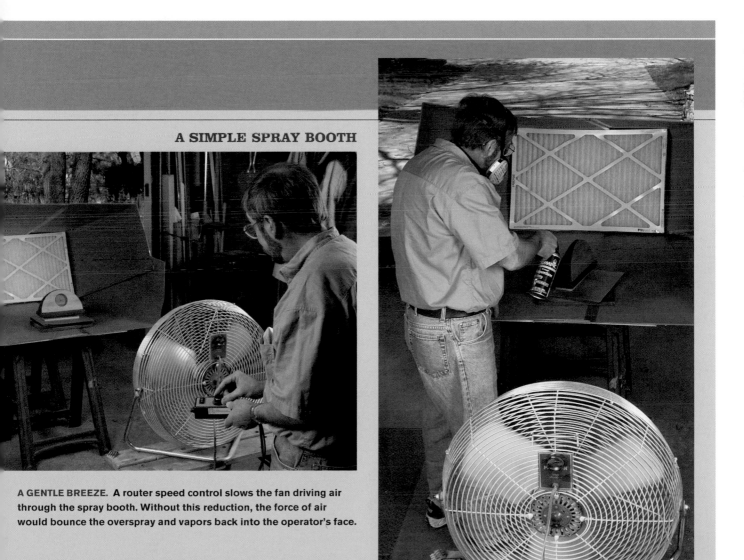

A SIMPLE SPRAY BOOTH

A GENTLE BREEZE. A router speed control slows the fan driving air through the spray booth. Without this reduction, the force of air would bounce the overspray and vapors back into the operator's face.

A MAKESHIFT SPRAY BOOTH. Made from a cardboard box and a furnace filter, this cheap and disposable spray booth is ideal for collecting overspray when using aerosols.

Spray Technique

The secret to achieving even coverage is keeping your wrist locked. Keep the can a steady 6 in. to 12 in. from and parallel to the workpiece. Don't let your wrist move the can in an arc.

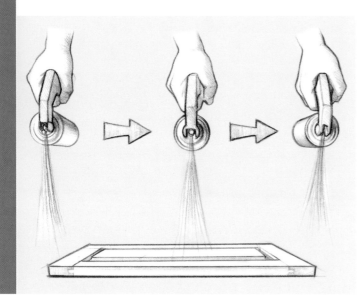

Apply Coats in Both Directions

To avoid streaking and missed areas, overlap each pass by 50%.

Spray another coat perpendicular to the first.

price. The warnings on the cans of aerosol finishes read something like this: "Contains propane, isobutane, and petroleum distillates. Vapor harmful. Do not puncture or incinerate. Exposure to heat or prolonged exposure to sun may cause bursting." Pay attention to these important warnings. That innocent-looking aerosol can is really a little bomb.

A few precautions will prevent disaster. When I use an aerosol finish, I always open a window or a garage door and turn on a fan behind me that sweeps air across the project toward the outside. The flow of fresh air keeps the fumes away from my face. I wear a good organic vapor respirator, too. While these precautions keep me from inhaling the vapors, they do nothing to

keep the overspray from sticking to everything in its path. My solution is to spray small projects inside a large cardboard box fitted with a furnace filter (see the right photo on p. 113). This easy-to-make, disposable booth collects overspray.

The shelf life of aerosol finishes varies: For lacquer and shellac it is almost indefinite, but with varnish the driers lose their effectiveness after about two years. With any can of finish of uncertain age, it is best to do a sample spray to make sure that it dries properly.

CHRIS A. MINICK is a consulting editor to *Fine Woodworking* magazine.

Better Painted Furniture

BY CHRIS A. MINICK

"If it works, don't mess with it," sums up the attitude that many woodworkers have toward finishing. Learning about a new finishing technique can be complicated and confusing. So it seems easier to stick with an old standby like tung oil, or stain followed by varnish, even though it may be merely adequate. If that's your habit, you may have overlooked an important class of finishes—paint.

Paint is a versatile medium because it can be used as a design accent to emphasize the lines of a piece, or it can be used to draw attention to handsome woods in furniture (see the photo on p. 116). A painted

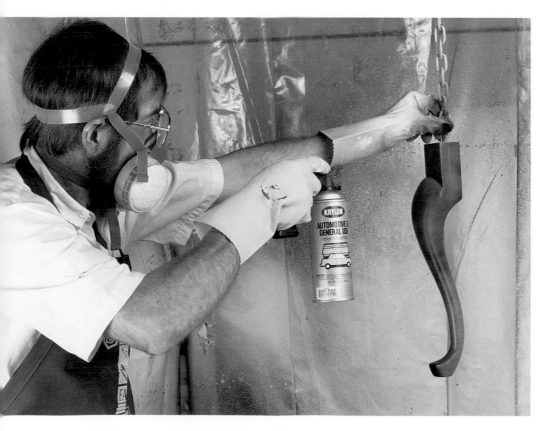

AUTOMOTIVE AEROSOL PAINT MAKES FOR A FLAWLESS FINISH. Wearing an organic-vapor respirator and rubber gloves, Chris Minick sprays a cabriole leg in a number of light coats. By hanging the leg from a chain, he can rotate the leg as he fills in missed areas. The spray booth is a U-shaped drape of 4-mil polyethylene hung from his garage rafters. Minick leaves the doors open for ventilation.

finish also lets you use up those too-good-to-burn pieces of scrapwood. But don't be mistaken. Paint cannot cover up poor workmanship or shoddy surfaces. A painted finish requires better preparation than a clear finish. Fortunately, there are some products that make the whole process relatively painless.

If I have to paint a fairly large project or one that needs a special color, I use a good latex paint and an airless sprayer. But for most items, especially the ones that require a professional-looking paint job (such as the coffee-table legs in the photo above), I use ordinary aerosol spray cans for priming, painting, and clear coating. Auto-parts stores have a marvelous variety of colors and types to choose from. And automotive fillers and putties are superb, too.

Learning From Automotive Finishers

Folks working in the automotive industry are constantly refining paint finishes, due to the meticulous demands of car finishes (see the sidebar on the facing page). That's the main reason I buy many of my furniture-finishing products, including fillers, primers, and paints, from my auto-parts store. And given the fact that paint is more easily scratched and more difficult to repair than most clear finishes, I borrow another technique from automobile finishers: I clear coat my painted finishes. Before I buy anything for a project, though, I think through my whole painting strategy.

Planning Your Paint Job

Painting, like any finishing technique, can be frustrating when some unexpected problem arises halfway through the process. The best way to eliminate surprises is to test all your materials and practice new techniques on scrapwood. After all, you wouldn't cut dovetails the first time using prized wood for your project. So you should treat paint finishing the same way. Paint decisions for a piece of furniture must be made before the first board is cut.

Because my furniture pieces often combine painted elements as well as stained and clear-coated portions, it's easier to finish each component separately, then assemble them. Though this requires careful planning of the construction and care in final assembly, it eliminates complicated masking and leads to better finish results.

When choosing stock for your project, think about which components will require special needs. For example, if you decide that certain parts must be real smooth, then maple, poplar, and birch are good wood choices. However, if you want to show a bit of wood texture through the paint, then open-grained woods, such as oak and ash, are more appropriate. I wanted smooth, glossy black legs on my coffee table that would enhance the figured-mahogany veneer top and apron. In addition, I wanted the legs to be hard to guard against knocks. For these reasons, maple was the logical wood choice. But as far as the painting goes, the wood used is irrelevant, really, as long as you are careful with the under-paint treatments.

Why New Car Finishes Work on Wood

Furniture makers may question the wisdom of using automotive finishes on wood. After all, aren't car finishes brittle—meant for relatively immobile surfaces like metal instead of dimensionally unstable substrates like wood? Although that argument was true in the past, it is no longer accurate. Automotive primers, aerosol paints, clear-coat finishes, and touch-up paints have changed because car components have changed. The latest materials, such as high-impact plastics and composites, are used to manufacture car bumpers, trim, and door panels. So paint makers have had to reformulate their coatings to accommodate increasing flexibility. This flexibility allows woodworkers to use car-finishing products on wood, which is notoriously unstable. If you don't care to use finishes from the auto-parts store, you can use most general-purpose aerosol primers, paints, and clear coatings to get equally stunning results.

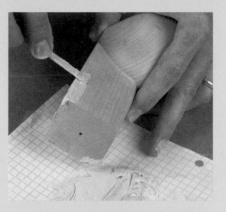

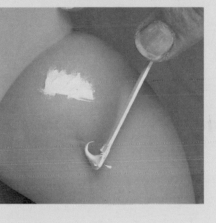

TWO-PART AUTO-BODY FILLER WON'T SHRINK, so it's great for leveling defects in wood. Using plastic-covered graph paper to measure the proper amount of filler and catalyst, Minick mixes the filler. After he packs the filler, he uses a knife to strike the repair flush with the surface, which will reduce sanding later. Areas of the leg that will be glued have been masked off. The filler cures quickly.

GLAZING PUTTY SMOOTHS OUT BLEMISHES IN PRIMER. After Minick primes a leg, he sands it out to reveal tiny surface dents and nicks, which he fills with blue glazing putty. When that's dry, he'll sand, reprime, and then lightly sand again in preparation for paint.

Preparing Surfaces and Equipment

The key to getting flawless painted furniture is meticulous surface preparation. The monochromatic nature of paint dramatically magnifies minor flaws that would otherwise go unnoticed under a clear finish. Small tearouts, hairline cracks in knots, stray sanding scratches, and other seemingly minor defects must be filled and smoothed before painting. This may sound like lots of dismal work, but if you follow car surface-preparation steps, you can reduce the drudgery.

Sanding and filling All parts should be thoroughly sanded to at least 180 grit and inspected under a strong light; then use auto-body fillers to level off any voids. These polyester fillers (familiar brands include Bondo® and White Knight™) work exceptionally well at repair because they tenaciously stick to raw wood, cure quickly, sand easily, and accept most kinds of oil-based and latex primers and paint. Best of all, they don't shrink. On the downside, they smell bad and have a short working life once mixed, usually less than 15 minutes.

For the coffee-table legs, I filled dents and nicks with two-part auto-body filler (3M®'s 2K Lightweight Putty). I even built out an edge that had been clipped off on the bandsaw (see the top photo on above). I

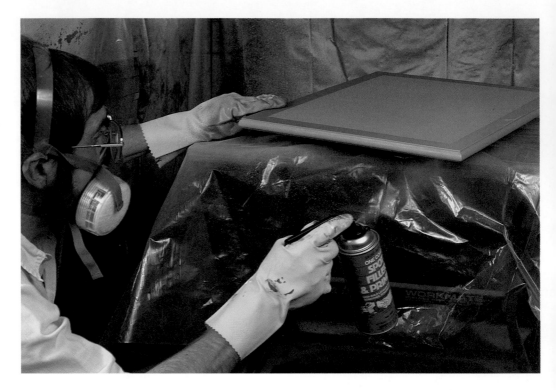

also filled in the knots. No matter how sound they look, knots always have cracks that show through the paint. Knots often contain resins, too, especially in softwoods. So once the filler in the knots had cured (about 30 minutes), I sanded it flush and spot-sealed the knots with shellac just to be safe. Finally, to make the edges of the medium-density fiberboard (MDF) top perfectly smooth, I used some spackle (see sidebar on the facing page).

Setting up a makeshift spray booth I don't have a paint booth in my home shop, so before I prime or paint, I set up a crude but effective painting area in my garage (see the photo on p. 115). Ventilation for my plastic spray booth is provided by a box fan that draws outside air through an open rear door and exhausts it through a partially opened garage door. I also use a good organic-vapor respirator to protect myself when I'm using aerosol cans to spray primer and high-solvent lacquers.

Priming and puttying Primers serve the same functions for painted finishes as sealers do under clear coats. Primers seal in resins and extractives that may discolor the paint, provide a uniform nonporous base for the color coat, and highlight any defects that were missed in the filling process. Aerosol primers are sensible to use if you're painting relatively small areas. I often use automotive high-build, scratch-filling primers under pigmented-lacquer paints. High-build primers are easy to apply, sand like a dream, and fill in tiny nicks and pits in wood. Adhesion tests in my shop show that automotive primers are completely compatible with high-solvent lacquers, but marginally compatible with oil paints and not at all with latex. When I buy primer at the store, I pick up several different brands of cans and shake each until I hear the little agitator ball dislodge. I pick the can that takes the longest for the ball to loosen because, generally, this means the primer contains a higher percentage of solids. Primers with more solids do a better job and are easier to sand.

Allow the primer to dry thoroughly (it should powder easily when sanded), and then inspect the piece carefully. You'll be surprised at the number of imperfections that will appear on your supposedly smooth wood. You must fill the tiny defects, or they'll show through the paint. Don't use the two-part auto filler this time, though, because it won't stick to the prime coat. Instead, use an automotive glazing putty, which is designed for application over primer (see the bottom photo on p. 117). 3M®'s Acryl-Blue Glazing Putty suits my needs, but any nonshrinking brand should work.

Sand the primer and dried putty smooth. Next apply a final coat of primer. Then sand again—this time to at least 220 grit but not finer than 320-grit. While you're sanding, be careful not to cut through to the wood, or you will have to reprime. The object of this final sanding is to level and smooth the surface but still leave some tiny scratches in the primer. This slight texture, called tooth, makes a better bond between the primer and top coat.

Use Spackle to Fill Voids in Edges

The MDF edges of my coffee-table top posed a unique finishing problem for me. Because the top was veneered, I needed a way to hide the MDF core. Edge-banding with solid wood was an option, but that didn't fit my design. I ruled out veneer as well because of the shaped edge that I wanted. So I decided to paint the edges black, like the legs. But first I had to prepare the surface of the MDF for primer.

MDF absorbs finish like a sponge, and the small pits in the core must be filled or they will show through the paint. A few finishers tackle this problem by using glazing coats; this technique requires real skill. Large furniture manufacturers solve the problem by spraying on two-part edge filler/surfacer, but it is expensive, is hard to find, and requires specialized spray equipment. I avoided all this by wiping a coat of wallboard spackling compound (made by DAP®) on the exposed MDF edges (see the photo at right). The spackle sands easily, fills the pits, and provides a good base for the primer. To save yourself some work, mask off the top and bottom of the tabletop before you start spackling the edges.

SPACKLE FILLS VOIDS IN MEDIUM-DENSITY FIBERBOARD. After masking off the veneered top of his table with paper and acrylic adhesive tape, the author rubs wallboard spackle onto the MDF edges. The spackle adheres well, dries quickly, and sands beautifully.

FOR A HIGH-GLOSS FINISH, rub out the clear coats with liquid automotive polishing compound. As a finishing touch, Minick buffs out the clear-lacquer top coat (one of five) on a coffee-table leg.

Painting, Clear Coating, and Rubbing Out

Aerosol paint cans are available in different colors, gloss levels and brands. I have had good luck using both Plasti-Kote® and Krylon® on furniture. Aerosol paints that are low-gloss sand easier than high-gloss ones, but I prefer the high-gloss variety because their higher resin content adds to the durability of the finish. You shouldn't be overly concerned about the actual glossiness, however, because the final sheen of the project will be controlled by the clear coat.

To start painting, I mist a tack coat of paint over all the primed area. Then I spray several light coats to fill in the blanks until the entire surface is covered with a level wet coat. Continued painting at this point will result in runs or sags. Let the solvent evaporate for 5 minutes or so, and then lay on another coat the same way. Two or three coats are usually enough to provide sufficient color build on a well-primed substrate.

For the tabletop's edge, I overcoated the spackled and sanded edge with the same automotive primer and paint that I used for the legs. The only differences were that I masked off the top and then used a lazy Susan to hold the work (see the photo on p. 118).

The clear coat is the final touch that sets apart an average paint job from a real show-stopper. Clear coats not only protect the paint from occasional dings but also add depth to the finish, which is more suitable for fine furniture. In addition, clear coats unify components by providing a consistent sheen over the entire piece. And clear coats are easier to rub out and repair than paint.

For peace of mind, I usually choose my clear finish from the same resin family as the paint. I used an aerosol automotive clear acrylic on my table project, but any good clear lacquer will work. For the tabletop edges, I clear coated the paint with Pratt & Lambert® #38, which is the same varnish I used on the mahogany-veneered top and apron. Four or more clear coats may be needed to achieve a good film thickness (3 mils to 4 mils). Remember, some film will be lost when rubbing out, so compensate for this. Make sure that your paint is completely dry before you clear coat. I like to wait several days.

For rubbing out clear coats to a high luster, I like to use liquid automotive buffing compounds (not paste compounds). I've found that car buffing compounds are easier to use than those carried by most wood-finishing-supply places. Both 3M and Meguiar's® offer good compounds for polishing. Meguiar's has several formulas with different abrasive levels for hand rubbing or power buffing. Let the clear coats dry a day or so, and then buff out to whatever sheen you desire (see the photo above).

CHRIS A. MINICK is a consulting editor to *Fine Woodworking* magazine.

Three Steps to a Flawless Painted Finish

BY PAUL SNYDER

a series of preparation and priming steps that get the surface of the piece progressively smoother.

Because the wood will be hidden under paint, it doesn't make sense to use expensive furniture-grade hardwoods, such as oak, ash, walnut, and mahogany. Poplar, MDF, birch plywood, pine, and paint-grade alder and maple are more suitable for painting. Paint grade just means the wood has grain or color variations that make it unsuitable for a clear or stained finish.

I f you associate the word *paint* with images of a pail of house paint, a roller, and a brush, you may have difficulty linking it to fine furniture. However, painted built-in cabinets, bookcases, wall units, and furniture are as popular today as they have ever been, and a great paint job stands comparison with the best clear finish.

There is more to achieving a quality painted finish than meets the eye, and the process is different than obtaining a clear finish. Much of the effort centers on the need for a perfectly flat, smooth base for the paint. To get this base, I work through

Surface Preparation Is Critical

Getting the wood ready for painting is even more important than preparing it for a clear finish, despite the fact that any repairs will be hidden under the paint. The first step is to inspect all of the surfaces and fill any holes, cracks, and gaps, then remove any glue runs or drips.

Once the filler is dry (for more on the different types of fillers, see the sidebar on p. 122), sand the wood with P150-grit paper. This grade of paper levels the surface

1. PREPARATION

2. PRIMING

3. PAINTING

1. Preparation: A Filler for Every Blemish

Fillers under a painted finish don't need to blend into the wood, but they shouldn't shrink as they dry, leaving a low spot that must be refilled. Use fillers that are easy to sand. I also prefer fillers that dry fast.

Some of the best painted finishes are on cars, and auto-supply shops sell fillers that will help you achieve such quality. For fine cracks, flat end grain, and flat MDF edges, automotive spot and glazing putty works well.

Spackle is a good choice on flat or routed end grain and MDF profiles. However, spackle shouldn't be used to fill a deep hole; sanding it can leave a depression in the surface of the piece. Spackle also dries a lot more slowly than other fillers, so use it sparingly.

A SMOOTH SURFACE. Large holes are best filled with an auto-body filler that must be mixed with a hardener (above). Fast-drying wood filler is ideal for medium-size holes (center right).

and makes it uniform, but leaves it relatively rough so that the primer still has some "tooth" to latch on to. As you sand each surface, start with any areas that were filled; excess filler will create a high spot that will show up later in the finish. However, filler used in large holes might shrink, leaving a recess that will need to be filled and sanded again.

Pay attention to end grain, edges, and profiles End grain will soak up a lot of primer if you don't pretreat it. Either seal end grain with glue size, shellac, glazing putty, or spackle and then sand it smooth;

or sand the edges with P220- or higher-grit sandpaper to burnish the surface, which will prevent the primer from soaking in too deeply.

On routed profiles, the aim is to achieve a smooth surface but still retain the crispness of the profile. Automotive glazing putty dries too fast, and glue size is relatively difficult to sand; like shellac, glue size doesn't fill the many small voids that cause a rough texture. I've found that the best filler for profiles is spackle (for more on using spackle, see "Tips for MDF" below) because it is easy to use and easy to shape when dry.

Tips for MDF

When MDF is cut or routed, a rough, porous surface is exposed. The best way to fill and smooth it is to cover the area with spackle, and then use a small, dampened brush with the bristles cut short to work the excess spackle out of the corners and curves before it has a chance to harden. Once the spackle dries, smooth it with a sanding sponge that can be shaped to fit into the profile.

Avoid using a water-based primer on MDF, which can cause the fibers to swell and leave the surface bumpy. Instead, choose an oil-based primer or alcohol-based shellac.

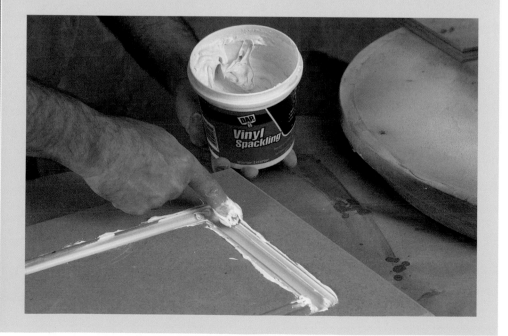

Select a compatible primer with the top coats and adhere well to both the wood and the top coats. The primer also should fill the grain, leaving the surface flat, as well as dry quickly and sand easily. If you'll be using a water-based top coat, choose a 100 percent acrylic primer.

There are situations when another type of primer is preferred. On areas prone to staining—wood knots, sap streaks, tannins, and pitch—shellac is the best choice. To simply seal the wood, use clear shellac, but to seal and prime the wood, use pigmented shellac such as Zinnser's BIN®.

If the paint you're using contrasts a lot with white primer, tint the primer to a color close to the paint. The paint will obscure the tinted primer with fewer coats, and if the finish is scratched or otherwise damaged, the primer will be less visible.

Spackle is especially well suited for filling mitered corners in crown molding, where the detail and location call for a filler that can be spread easily and then sanded.

Break the corners for a better surface

The final preparation is to lightly sand the sharp corners, rounding them over slightly. Known as breaking the corners, this step helps paint flow from a flat surface onto a corner, avoiding paint buildup. It also reduces the chances of sanding through the primer on the corners.

Primer Readies a Smooth Surface for the Topcoats

With the obvious defects filled, everything sanded, and the corners broken, it's time to prime. Don't think of primer as being optional; it's indispensable for the flat, smooth base necessary for a painted finish. Primer performs a variety of functions that either the paint itself doesn't do or the primer does better.

The first coat of primer may be absorbed unevenly—Apply an even coat of primer. With MDF and maple, one coat of primer often is all that's needed because the substrate is dense and free of pores. Other woods usually take two coats and sometimes three.

Despite the extra preparation on end grain and profiles, these areas still may absorb an excess of primer. The natural instinct is to apply it more heavily to get continuous, even coverage. But applying primer thickly leads to sags and runs and also slows the drying time. A better option is to apply primer in several thin coats until you get uniform coverage.

Once the primer dries, it's time to find and fix all of the surface flaws that this first

APPLY THE FIRST COAT OF PRIMER. Brush on an even coat. On areas that will absorb the primer, let this coat dry and then apply a second coat.

FILL SMALL BLEMISHES. The first coat of primer reveals surface imperfections that may have been missed during the initial preparation.

SAND THE PRIMER. Depending on how rough the surface is, sand the first coat of primer using P150-grit or P220-grit paper on a random-orbit sander. A sanding sponge is a good choice for smoothing moldings.

coat has revealed. Each little hole, crack, and other imperfection that you didn't see during the surface preparation stands out clearly after the first coat of primer.

Filling, sanding, and applying the next coat of primer If you need to make minor repairs, and you are working with MDF or a tight-grained wood such as maple, sand the whole surface carefully after the filler dries; use P220 grit on a sanding block or a random-orbit sander. If the primer has soaked in a lot, or if there's a strong grain pattern, the entire surface will need a vigorous sanding, which means you may end up removing most of the primer. If the grain is visible, use P150 grit, sanding until either the wood begins to show through the primer or all the shiny dimples (low spots) on the surface disappear. Use a random-orbit sander on large, flat areas, but on narrow boards, molding, or inside cor-

ners, use a sanding sponge. To avoid cutting through the edges and corners on narrow pieces, fold the sponge to fit the width.

With everything sanded, remove the dust and feel the surface with your fingers. Sand any rough areas again as needed. If there are bare spots, prime and sand them again. Then apply a second coat of primer over the entire surface. Sand this additional coat with P220-grit paper and a fine sanding sponge, working carefully to avoid cutting through the primer. When you're finished, remove the dust and inspect the surface to make sure all of the problem areas have been addressed. The surface should look as defect-free as you want the final painted finish to look. If you sanded through to bare wood, prime and sand only those areas again.

Two Tinted Top Coats are Protected by a Clear Coat

Now that all of the hard work is done, it's time to paint. If more than a day has passed since you last sanded the primed surfaces, go over them quickly and lightly with P220-grit sandpaper. Like other finishes, primer continues to cure for a number of days, so the sanding scratches tend to shrink and close, reducing the bond between primer and paint.

If the paint is tinted and you have more than one can, mix them all together in an empty paint bucket to ensure the same color throughout the job. Then pour the paint into a smaller container with a large opening until it's half full. Dip the brush into the paint no more than halfway up the bristles, and gently tap them on the inside wall of the container to remove excess paint.

Brush with the grain in long strokes, holding the paintbrush at about a 45 degree angle to the surface. Overlap strokes slightly to maintain a wet edge, and apply light pressure to keep all of the bristles in contact with the surface. Pull up as you reach the

Seal Before Priming

I use a clear sealer when I'm painting a piece that's made of wood suitable for a stained or clear-coat finish (e.g., pine). Applying the sealer makes it easier to strip paint from the piece if someone ever wants to change the look; it's hard to remove every last trace of the pigments when primer or paint is applied to bare wood. An alternative to alcohol-based shellac is a water-based shellac such as Ultra-Seal from Target® Coatings. It can be sprayed safely and cleans up with warm, soapy water.

3. Painting: Pay Top Dollar for the Topcoat

Paint for interior cabinetry and furniture should be formulated to resist sags and runs, and it should dry fast to avoid excessive dust collection. It also should provide a completely opaque finish after two coats and be durable enough for the intended use of the piece. Don't be tempted to economize with a $15 can of paint from a home center; quality is indicated by price, so be prepared to pay upwards of $30 per gallon for paint used by the pros.

There are a number of quality 100% acrylic and acrylic-enamel house paints. Generally speaking, manufacturers use the term enamel to describe any paint that has a smooth, hard surface. Add a few ounces of Floetrol, a latex paint additive that improves flow-out and leveling, to each gallon you use.

A good paint deserves a good brush. Pay extra for a quality nylon brush with flagged ends (the bristle ends are split). Nylon is softer than polyester or polyester/nylon blends and will help the paint lay down more smoothly with fewer brush-stroke ridges. The flagged ends will leave a finer, smoother pattern.

TRY TO PAINT HORIZONTALLY. It is easier to get a good finish with no sags or runs if you paint surfaces when they are horizontal.

Paints Designed for Spraying

Spraying is the quickest and easiest way to get a smooth, high-quality finish. I use high-volume, low-pressure (HVLP) spray equipment and select a paint designed for spray application. A couple of good brands are Target Coatings and M.L. Campbell.

CHOOSE THE RIGHT BRUSH. Use a 2-in. or 2½-in. angled brush to get into small or confined areas (above). Switch to a 3-in. brush for large panels (right), and apply the paint in long, flowing strokes.

SAND BETWEEN COATS. Use a fine sanding sponge to smooth the first top coat. Don't worry about sanding through to the primer in some spots; it is more important to get a smooth surface.

end of a stroke to avoid leaving a ridge. On long surfaces where you need to apply the paint in sections, start a new section just beyond the last strip and brush back into the wet section. Starting in the wet section causes pooling.

Plan to use two coats of paint. Trying to obtain 100 percent coverage with one coat encourages applying the paint too thickly.

Scuff-sand between coats to promote good adhesion, and allow the paint to dry for at least two weeks to reach optimal durability before putting the piece to use.

Clear coat the paint. After letting the second coat of paint dry for 24 hours, you can apply a coat of clear finish for improved durability, added depth, and optional sheen adjustment.

The texture of the painted surface and the final sheen determine how much sanding is needed before the clear coat. If the surface is flat and you're planning on a satin or semigloss clear coat, then a light scuff-sanding is fine. If there are substantial brush ridges, or if you want a high gloss, the paint should be sanded until it is level.

For hand-sanding, use sanding sponges. Their padding helps to avoid cutting through the paint. For larger flat surfaces, Mirka's Abralon® abrasive pads can be attached to a random-orbit sander to make the job faster.

To minimize changes in color, the clear coat should be completely clear, non-yellowing, and compatible with the paint. A water-based polyurethane is a good choice. You will be rewarded with a painted finish every bit as attractive as the finest clear finish.

PAUL SNYDER is a professional finisher near Fredericksburg, Virginia.

Glazing With Polyurethane

BY
M. DAVID BECTON

I like the look of a glazed finish. It gives wood a color and depth that's hard to match. So I developed a simple glazing method using polyurethane varnish. By using polyurethane varnish, I am able to create a durable, hard finish that has excellent resistance to heat, moisture, and solvents. And it can be wiped on with little fuss, a nice advantage for anyone without spray equipment. I use a mineral-spirits-based clear, satin, gel-polyurethane varnish. Bartley (see "Sources" on p. 136) makes one called "gel varnish" that works well.

In addition to great depth, there are several other good reasons for choosing a glazed finish to color wood. It's a great way to darken light-colored areas of sapwood in a board. Then, too, you can darken or lighten an entire project to suit your taste. Also, blotchy areas can be blended out. And finally, glazing allows you to tame any wild grain, and it's just about foolproof.

With this method there aren't a lot of hard-and-fast rules, so each step can be customized as needed to get the finish color and depth you want. Usually a sealer coat,

Glazing from Start to Finish

Adding layers of polyurethane glaze to a cherry porringer table, the author trans-formed the unfinished piece (top) into a table with deep, rich, warm colors (bottom).

SAND. To achieve a smooth, glazed finish, hardwoods, like this cherry, should be sanded through 180 grit.

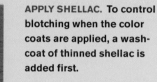

APPLY SHELLAC. To control blotching when the color coats are applied, a wash-coat of thinned shellac is added first.

ADD STAIN. The author wanted a yellow tint, so he added a coat of golden oak stain.

FIRST GLAZE COAT. A poly-urethane gel provides the first coat of glaze. The author used Bartley's golden oak gel stain.

SECOND GLAZE COAT. For an aged and weathered look, a 50-50 mix of two polyurethane gels—walnut and clear—is applied.

THE TOP COAT. A clear top coat adds depth to the fin-ish, plus the top coat pro-vides some extra abrasion protection.

typically thinned shellac, is applied to the bare wood. Then, depending upon the color you're looking for, a coat of stain may be added. The glazing coats follow: usually one to three of them, but there can be more. These colored coats are sometimes the same color, but the colors in each coat are typically changed as needed to achieve the final color. As a last step, a clear top coat is added to help protect the glaze.

Coloring the Polyurethane

To add color to a gel-polyurethane finish, mix in Japan colors, universal tints, or even artist's oil colors. Most oil-based paints also work. But to avoid drying problems, don't mix more than one part coloring agent to eight parts gel–polyurethane.

Another good option, and one I used for the porringer table shown here, is to mix in one of the gel-stain products made by Bartley. Bartley's gel products can be mixed in any proportion.

As you might expect, matching the glaze to your desired color is a matter of trial and error. It's best to work with small amounts while trying to nail down the color. Also, jot down notes on the proportions of gel and color that were used so that you'll be able to achieve the same color again.

One more point here. It would be prudent to do all of the finishing steps first on a test board. That way you'll be able to look at the test board and see whether the final result is what you want.

Preparing the Surface

BRUSH ON SHELLAC. A washcoat of thinned shellac added before the stain helps control blotching.

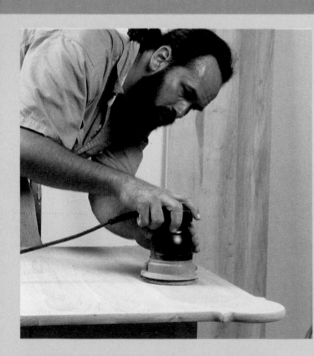

THE FIRST STEP IS TO SAND THOROUGHLY. Don't rush the sanding process. A little extra time here pays dividends later.

APPLY THE STAIN. To help achieve the result you want, the wood-coloring process starts with a coat of oil-based stain; golden oak was used for the porringer table.

If you're unhappy with the look of a glaze coat as it is being applied (and before it dries), simply wet a paper towel or rag with mineral spirits and wipe off the entire coat. Then, with the slate clean, make adjustments in the color and try again. And the coat underneath won't be affected. Sometimes it can take several adjustments until you get the color you want.

Surface Preparation Is Critical

If I've learned one thing in 20 years of finishing, it's that the quality of the sanding process on bare wood can make or break the quality of the final product. Heavy mill marks can be removed with 80-grit sandpaper. For lighter mill marks, use 100-grit paper followed by 120 grit. Depending on the hardness of the wood and how rich a finish you want, you might use an even finer grit, say 180 or higher.

Once the sanding has been completed, brush on a washcoat of shellac to all the surfaces. The shellac prevents the stain from splotching and streaking.

Dewaxed shellac works very well, but white or amber shellac may also be used. Keep in mind that each coat of shellac adds some color, usually a very light amber.

For hardwoods, like the cherry used in the porringer table, use one part 3-lb.-cut shellac and one part denatured alcohol to get a 1½-lb. cut. For softwoods, the mix should be thinner; one part 3-lb.-cut shellac and three parts alcohol. As you apply the shellac, try to avoid overlapping the brush strokes. That way, you won't spread too much shellac in one area.

After the shellac washcoat dries, cut down any nibs—crystallized dust and raised grain that dry in the finish—with 220-grit sandpaper. Silicon-carbide paper, used dry, is my usual weapon here. By taking a little extra time to get a nice, even washcoat, the subsequent coats of finish will go on easier and more consistently.

Applying the Glaze

A CLOTH PAD helps control the application of the glaze coats. The pad is made from a couple of rectangular-shaped pieces of an old cotton T-shirt. Wrap one piece around a folded piece to create a soft pad that will fit comfortably in your hand.

THE FIRST COAT OF GLAZE. A brush is used to apply the first glaze coat, a gel stain. The cloth pad allows the author to remove just the right amount of glaze from the surface to get the desired result.

Stain the Surface, if Needed

At this point, start the coloring process by applying a light to medium shade of stain. Because I wanted the porringer table to have a yellow tint, I used a single coat of Minwax golden oak stain. Had I been looking for a brown tint, I would have used Minwax provincial stain. But don't feel locked in by what I do. You can use any color of oil-based stain that gets you toward the final desired color. However, if a stain isn't going to help you achieve the color you want, simply skip this step.

Apply the stain with a brush, then wipe off the excess with a soft rag. When working on a flat surface, like a tabletop, flood the wood with stain. Then use the brush to work in the liquid before removing the excess with the rag. You can remove either a little or a lot of the stain. For better control, it's best to apply the stain to one section at a time. Start with the least conspicuous area and then move to the most conspicuous.

One final point on stains—give them plenty of drying time, especially alkyd stains, which need 24 to 48 hours to dry completely. Rush this step, and you're simply begging for adherence problems with the polyurethane coats that will follow.

Apply the Glaze Coats

Once the shellac and stain coats have been completed, you're ready to start the glazing steps. The glaze is simply brushed on, then wiped off with a cloth pad. Using a pad to wipe off the glaze helps control the application better than a brush can.

The pad is made from a couple pieces of an old cotton T-shirt. One piece is cut into a rectangle, then a smaller piece is folded and placed inside the rectangle. When the rectangle is wrapped around the inner piece, the result is a nice, soft pad—much like a French polishing pad—that fits comfortably in your hand.

First coat The first coat of glaze is the foundation for all of the remaining coats. Subsequent coats simply build on the first coat.

The secret to the glazing steps is to go slowly and work only one area at a time. Brush on the glaze kind of thick and then, depending on the desired look, either wipe off just about all of it or leave most of it on. And don't try to get to the final color in one coat. Several lightly colored coats look better than one dark coat.

For the cherry porringer table, I used a single coat of Bartley's golden oak gel stain, wiping off the stain lightly with the pad. But you can choose any color oil-based gel stain you want. Or you can add color to a clear gel.

Adjusting the Tone

MIX THE SECOND COAT. The author wanted a "dirty" color, like that found on many antiques, so he mixed walnut gel stain and clear gel-polyurethane finish. Japan colors, universal tints, artist's oils and oil-based paints are other good options for coloring polyurethane gels.

Sanding After this and all subsequent coats of glaze have fully dried, you need to do a little light sanding to smooth out the tiny nibs left in the dried finish. This sanding step also helps level out any uneven brush strokes.

Sanding between coats has an added benefit of leaving a better surface for the next coat to grab. Unlike lacquer, polyurethane does not melt into the coat below it, so the sanding scratches create a foothold for the new coat.

I find that 400-grit to 1,000-grit wet sandpaper dipped in soapy water does a nice job. But it's important to sand with a light touch. The first coat is thinner than paper, so it won't take much sanding to cut through it.

Be sure to remove all of the sanding dust completely before you add the next coat of glaze. If you don't, the new glaze coat will trap the dust particles on the surface. A good going-over with a vacuum will remove most of the dust. Then wipe it down with a tack rag to pick up the rest.

Second coat Once the first coat has been sanded, it's time to apply color to the gel. But before starting, you'll need to make another cloth pad, because there's more brushing and wiping to do.

I wanted the porringer table to appear aged and weathered. The idea was to have the finish look almost dirty from many years of service. And to do that I needed a dark color, one that was almost black. So I

BRUSH ON THE SECOND COAT. A heavy coat of glaze is applied with a brush, then it's partially wiped off with the cloth pad. Less is wiped off in areas that need to be darkened.

YOU CAN'T GO WRONG HERE. If the color of a glaze coat isn't what you wanted, simply wipe it off before it dries, remix the colors, and try again.

Sources

Bartley

800-787-2800

www.bartleycollection.com

Wood Finishing Supplies

800-451-0678

www.woodfinishingsupplies.com

added Bartley's walnut stain, mixing one part stain to one part Bartley's clear gel. This mixture tends to be thick, though, so I usually add thinner until the blend becomes about the consistency of cake batter.

If the wood surface has a fairly consistent color throughout, you can simply brush on the glaze and wipe it off as needed. Try to avoid putting it on so heavy that you end up with raised brush marks. It should flow smoothly and lie flat on the surface.

If the glaze is globbing up the surface with streaky color, you're probably putting on too much. Try applying a lighter coat. To make the rag glide just right, it's sometimes helpful to thin the glaze with mineral spirits or Penetrol®. But keep in mind that thinning the polyurethane mixture is also going to dilute the binding qualities. That means it won't adhere as well to the previ-

ous coat. So don't add more than one part glaze to one part thinner.

If there are light and dark areas you'd like to even out, use the glaze to darken the light areas. Then decide how much glaze, if any, you need to add to the dark zones.

If you don't like the color you're seeing as it's applied, just wipe it off with a paper towel or rag, wetted with mineral spirits. Then adjust the color and try again.

Let each coat dry thoroughly. If you don't, and you need to wipe off the next coat, you are probably going to remove both coats instead of just one. In most areas of the country, a glaze coat will dry overnight, but in Georgia, where it can get pretty humid, I generally wait a little longer.

Additional glaze coats The long drying time between each of the coats has one advantage. It gives you plenty of time to

Adding the Clear Top Coat

MIX THE TOP COAT. Once all of the glaze coats have been added, a topcoat is prepared using clear gel-polyurethane that has been thinned with mineral spirits or Penetrol. The mixture should have the consistency of 30-weight motor oil.

WIPE ON A TOP COAT. The top coat brings out all of the color and depth in the layers of glaze.

study the evolving color and depth of the finish and decide whether the color of the next glaze coat needs to be darkened, lightened, or perhaps changed entirely.

In most cases, you'll be able to get the color and depth you need with just the first coat of glaze, plus two or three additional coats. For the porringer table, I added two coats on top of the first coat.

A Clear Top Coat for Depth

A clear top coat will give the layers of colored finish some additional depth. Plus, the top coat offers a little more scratch protection.

For small projects, I like to use Deft's polyurethane finish. It comes in a spray can for easy application and has a thin consistency, so it doesn't look quite so thick after it has dried.

On projects that are too big to be easily finished with a spray can, I apply clear gel-polyurethane thinned slightly with Penetrol. First I sand the surface thoroughly with 1,500-grit paper dipped in soapy water. Then I rub on the gel with a clean cloth pad.

I usually don't apply a top coat to all of the surfaces of a project. Instead, it's applied only to large, horizontal surfaces that tend to catch your eye quickly and stand out. So, on the porringer table, only the tabletop got the top coat.

Buffing Adds a Rich Luster

I could stop at this point and be more than satisfied with the results. But I prefer to include another step: buffing the finish. And like the top coat, this step is used only on tabletops and similar horizontal surfaces. All that's needed here is some buffing paste. I like a product made by 3M called Finesse-It ® (ebony). If not available locally, you can order it by mail through Wood Finishing Supplies (see "Sources"). This product is best used with an electric buffer and a wool

Coloring Sapwood

A band of sapwood can spoil an otherwise perfect panel. But coloring the panel with glaze produces a surface with an even tone.

polishing pad, but it can also be applied by hand with a cloth pad.

Work on a small section at a time. Start by applying a dab of the compound to the tabletop, then buff it out with the electric polisher or cloth pad. For the final step, use a soft rag to wipe off any of the compound remaining on the surface. It's a great way to polish the surface and to bring out all the color and depth of your glazed finish.

M. DAVID BECTON has been building and finishing furniture for 24 years. He lives in Americus, Georgia, where he operates a custom-furniture business.

Using Wood Bleach

BY JEFF JEWITT

PICK THE RIGHT BLEACH FOR THE JOB. These three types of wood bleach all have specific uses. No one bleach does it all.

My client's dining table had been damaged in a move, and two of its leaves were missing. The French-style reproduction table, about 60 years old, was veneered with a fruitwood that looked like cherry in grain and texture. But the wood had mellowed to a yellow-gold color. Cherry was the natural choice for the new leaves. But the color would be too red and would darken significantly over time.

I solved the problem with bleach. It removed the natural color of the cherry, providing me with a neutral background so I could match the original with a dye stain. The bleach also halted the darkening process in the cherry leaves, so the color of the table would remain uniform.

Matching old wood to new is only one application for wood bleaches. Most finishers are aware that bleaches remove unwanted stains—food, black water, and old dyes. But bleaches can do much more. They also even out tonal variations in dissimilar woods and produce blond or pickled finishes. The trick is knowing which bleach to use. For that, it helps to understand how wood bleach works (see "How Bleach Works" on pp.140–141).

For woodworkers, there are three general types of bleaches: peroxide, chlorine, and oxalic acid. All three work by altering the way wood molecules reflect light, thereby changing the color in the process. But each type of bleach is suited to particular tasks; they are not interchangeable.

Ideally, a bleach should work selectively to remove color, meaning that it should only remove the color that you want and not the color of anything around it. In most cases you'll need to experiment, especially if you don't know the composition of the stain. Because most bleaches are highly poisonous and often very corrosive to skin, you should always wear good rubber gloves, a dust mask (if you're mixing dry bleach powders), and safety glasses.

PEROXIDE BLEACHES WORK BEST at removing the natural color of the wood. This piece of mahogany veneer changed from a deep red to a light blond color with one application of peroxide bleach.

How Bleach Works

Color in an object is produced when the molecules selectively reflect light. These colored molecules may be organic, like those in dyes, or they can be inorganic, like those in pigments. Most bleaches, like peroxide and chlorine, work by disrupting the way that the molecules can reflect light. Other bleaches, like oxalic acid, convert the colored compound of a stain to a different, colorless one. The physics of these concepts may be difficult to understand, but the important thing to remember is that bleaches do not really remove the color of a substance. They simply change the material so it appears colorless.

As an example, tannic acid and ferrous sulfate, when dissolved in water, are colorless solutions. When mixed together, the two chemicals react and form a third compound, iron tannate, which is a grayish-black color. Iron tannate is the compound responsible for most of the black water spots on oak. When oxalic acid is added to this liquid, it converts the colored iron tannate molecules to iron oxalate, a colorless compound. When used in this respect, oxalic acid is a bleach.

Not every colored object can be bleached. Colors that are produced by inorganic molecules will not react to the bleach. Many pigments like carbon black (used in inks) and earth pigments (used in wood stains) will not react to bleach. These colors can only be completely removed by scraping or sanding the color off the surface of the wood.

Peroxide Bleaches Remove Natural Color

These bleaches are sold as two-part solutions, commonly labeled A and B. You'll find peroxide wood bleaches in most paint and hardware stores. The two chemicals are usually sodium hydroxide and a strong hydrogen peroxide solution. When used together, a powerful oxidizing reaction takes place that is effective in removing the natural color in wood, like the mahogany shown in the bottom photo on p. 139. To a lesser degree,

peroxide bleaches will lighten some woods that have been treated with pigment stains. They are ineffective on dye stains.

The most common way to apply this product is to wet the wood thoroughly with sodium hydroxide (part A) and immediately follow with hydrogen peroxide (part B). It's important with some tannin-rich woods like cherry and oak that part A not sit too long before part B is applied because the sodium hydroxide may darken the wood. You can also mix the two parts

CHLORINE BLEACHES REMOVE DYE STAINS. The natural color of walnut (left) is virtually unchanged by an application of chlorine bleach. But most of the dye stain on the birch veneer (right) has been removed with the same solution.

together and apply them at the same time, as long as you do this quickly after the parts are mixed. Usually one application is needed, but a second application may be necessary to even out the bleaching effect.

Some dark woods, like ebony, are not affected by peroxide bleaches. You can use this to your advantage if you want to bleach a tabletop with ebony inlay. On some woods, especially walnut, a greenish tinge may appear in some areas if the bleach is applied unevenly. To prevent this problem,

apply the bleach sparingly; use just enough to make the wood wet. Don't flood the surface.

Neutralize the alkaline effect of peroxide bleaches after the wood has dried by applying a weak acid, like white vinegar. Use one part vinegar to two parts water. Follow that with a clean water rinse.

Peroxide bleaches will remove all the natural color variations in wood, so use them judiciously. I use them to match sun-faded wood or to provide a neutral base for a decorative finish like pickled oak. You can also use them to compensate for heartwood/sapwood variations, but I usually prefer to bring the sapwood in line with the heartwood by hand coloring or spraying the sapwood with a dye stain.

Chlorine Bleaches Eliminate Dye Colors

Chlorine is a strong oxidizer that will remove or lighten most dye stains (see the right photo on p. 141). A weak chlorine-based laundry bleach such as Clorox® will work, but it will often take several applications to be effective. A much stronger solution can be made from swimming pool bleach—a dry chemical called calcium hypochlorite. It's inexpensive and can be purchased from a retailer of pool supplies.

The chief advantage of chlorine is that it will remove or lighten the dye without affecting the natural color of the wood. You can use laundry bleach or the stronger version—dry calcium hypochlorite powder mixed to a saturated solution in hot water. A saturated solution is created by adding the powder to water until no more powder will dissolve. Mix only in glass or plastic containers: The chemical will attack aluminum or steel. The mixture will lose its effectiveness if stored, so I make up only what I'll use right away. Cool to room temperature before using, and filter out solids.

Apply the solution liberally to the wood and, in some cases, the dye will immediately disappear. Some dyes may take longer to bleach, and some may only lighten but not disappear. Wait overnight to determine the full bleaching effect. If the color hasn't changed after two applications, applying more bleach won't help. You'll need to try another technique. Chlorine bleaches are usually ineffective on pigment-based stains. The only way to remove these are by sanding or scraping.

Oxalic Acid for Iron Stains and Weathering

Oxalic acid is unique in that it will remove a specific type of stain formed when iron and moisture come into contact with tannic acid. Some woods, like oak, cherry, and mahogany, naturally contain a high amount of tannic acid. A black stain results when the tannic acid reacts with water containing trace amounts of iron. Oxalic acid will remove this discoloration without affecting the natural color of the wood (see the photos on the facing page).

Oxalic acid also lightens the graying effects of outdoor exposure. It is the active ingredient in some deck brighteners. If used on furniture that has been stripped for refinishing, it will lighten the color and re-establish an even tone to the wood.

Iron-based stains are fairly easy to spot. They are grayish-black and usually ring-shaped. They may also show up as a splotchy appearance on oak that has been stripped. Before applying oxalic acid, remove any finish first.

In a plastic container, mix a solution from dry crystals of oxalic acid (available from most woodworking supply stores) in hot water. Allow the solution to cool to room temperature, and apply it to the entire surface, not just to the stain. Several applications may be needed with overnight drying in between. Once the surface of the wood is dry, any residual oxalic acid must be removed before sanding or finishing because the acid will damage subsequent finishes. Several water rinses will remove most of the oxalic acid crystals left on the wood surface. Neutralize the acidic wood surface with a solution made from one quart of water and two heaping tablespoons of baking soda. Then rinse off the baking-soda solution with water.

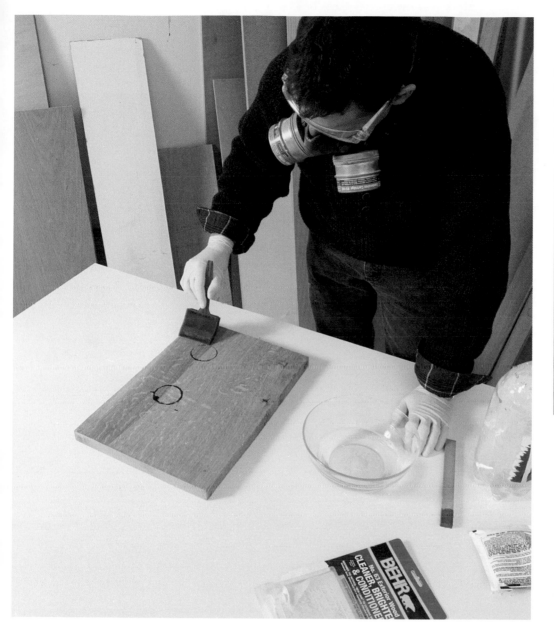

Solving Special Staining Problems

Stains that form on wood during the drying process are varied in their composition. Sticker stain, brown stain, streaking, and light "ghost" stains are all common problems. Some can be removed by bleach. The composition of the stain may be chemical or biological, so a trial-and-error approach may be needed when attempting to remove a stain. I often start with oxalic acid and then follow with chlorine. Peroxide bleaches are a last resort because the removal or acceptable lightening of the stain can result in bleaching the surrounding wood.

Stains like grape juice, tea, and fruits can be removed with a chlorine bleach. Remember to wipe the entire surface to get an even effect. Some blue and black inks with an iron base can be eliminated with oxalic acid, but carbon-based inks, like India ink, can't be removed by any bleach.

JEFF JEWITT restores furniture in Cleveland, Ohio, and is the author of *Taunton's Complete Illustrated Guide to Finishing* (2004).

The Quick, Modern Way to a Polished Finish

BY JEFF JEWITT

WET-SAND WITH WATER OR OIL. Either lubricant levels a finish and removes brush strokes or small bits of dust and debris. The author prefers rubbing oil thinned with mineral spirits.

The basic concept of rubbing out a finish is easy: Abrade the surface with very fine sandpaper to remove surface defects and level it out, then polish to the sheen you want. The old-world approach is to do this work by hand, using pumice and rottenstone, which work well but are time-consuming and physically exhausting to carry out. Some modern products simplify and speed up this process considerably. Combined with power-sanding and buffing equipment, these products deliver an efficient system for rubbing out a finish.

I prefer to wet-sand small surfaces, such as table aprons and legs, by hand. But I switch to air-powered equipment for larger areas, such as tabletops. The best tools for wet-sanding have opposing, in-line pads that vibrate back and forth in a straight-line motion, rather than making a circular scratch pattern. You can dry-sand some finishes, such as oil-based polyurethane and some lacquers, with an electric-powered

Creating a Satin Finish

WHAT YOU'LL NEED FOR A SATIN FINISH. After wet-sanding the surface by machine, the author accomplished the rest by hand, using 0000 steel-wool pads, Behlen's Wool-Lube and a little soapy water for lubrication. Then he rubbed the surface in long, even strokes to achieve a classic hand-rubbed finish.

STEEL-WOOL TIP: Improve the ergonomics of steel-wool pads. Unwrap 0000 steel-wool pads and refold them into quarters so that they will better fit your hand.

random-orbit sander as long as you use very fine (1,000 grit, or higher) stearated, or nonloading papers. Never use electric sanders when wet-sanding because of the risk of electric shock.

Start the process with the finest grit size that will remove the defects and level the finish. You can begin with 320-grit paper if the surface is badly orange-peeled or shows ridges from brush strokes. Or you can start with 800-grit or even 1,000-grit paper if you have only minimal surface problems

and you're shooting for a gloss finish in the end. I usually start with 400-grit or 600-grit silicon-carbide wet-or-dry sandpaper, and I use mineral oil cut 50 percent with mineral spirits as the lubricating medium for all of my oil- or lacquer-based finishes. I spray the mixture with a plant mister. Some people prefer to use water instead of oil. If you use water, add a small amount of dishwashing liquid as a lubricant.

I always work around the edges of a tabletop first, then move toward the center

Creating a Gloss Finish

BUFFING TIP: Smear it on, then buff it out. Use the buffer pad first to spread out the liquid compound, then tilt the pad slightly as you move it slowly over the surface. After buffing the surface in two directions, a deep gloss emerges from the surface of the finish.

USE COMPOUNDS IN A SEQUENCE OF GRITS. After wet-sanding the surface, the author buffed this table first with Meguiar's #1 medium-cut cleaner, then with #2 fine-cut cleaner. After that, he finished with #9 swirl remover to fill in the tiny hairline scratches left by the #2 cleaner.

(this routine helps me keep track of where I am), working in sequence up to at least 600-grit paper. If you're aiming for a gloss finish, work up to at least 800-grit or 1,000-grit paper. Sanding to a higher grit will speed up the polishing procedure later on.

If you want a classic, hand-rubbed satin finish, you can achieve the best results using steel wool and Wool-Lube (a rubbing lubri-

cant made by Behlen) or thinned wax (see the photos on p. 145). Squirt a couple of stripes of Wool-Lube on the surface, then mist it with soapy water. (I mix a capful of dishwashing liquid into a quart of water to clean up the mineral oil from the wet-sanding process.) Using moderate down-ward pressure, about 25 lbs. (you can practice by pushing down on a bathroom scale), rub the surface in straight strokes with the pad, following the direction of the grain. Repeat this process several times, then switch to a clean part of the steel-wool pad and rub the whole surface down again. Wipe the slurry off to check your progress. If you've done it right, the surface should look like brushed metal when viewed in backlighting.

If you are going for gloss, automotive compounds, available from auto-supply stores, offer a real innovation for polishing furniture finishes. Compounds are simply abrasive powders in liquid suspensions, or pastes. Two manufacturers, Meguiar's and 3M, offer products that work very well on wood finishes. They are used in stages to remove defects and scratches from wet-sanding. Some manufacturers sell a single product that breaks down into smaller grits as you use it, but I prefer using more than one compound. Because compound grit sizes vary, you should stick with products from a single manufacturer.

Beware—some buffing compounds create a whitish, hazy look on water-based lacquers. You may simply need to let the finish cure longer, but the haze is usually caused by solvents in the compound that soften the lacquer, making it hard to polish. If this happens, discontinue use of the compound and switch to a different one. (I've found that Meguiar's #10 plastic polish works well as the final polish for water-based finishes.)

You can use most rubbing compounds by hand, but for a large surface such as a dining-room table, a power buffer is the way to go. The most popular buffers are right-angle sander/polishers. If you purchase one, get a variable-speed buffer or a two-speed tool (rated at a maximum speed of 3,800 rpm). A polishing bonnet of either cotton or synthetic foam is attached to the buffer with a locking nut. Any bonnet can be cleaned, but to ensure efficient polishing, purchase a separate bonnet for each grade of compound that you use.

Polish the furniture in an area where flying compound won't be a problem, and wear an apron. Squirt a few stripes of compound across the surface, about 8 in. apart. With the buffer turned off, smear the compound all over the surface of the finish. Hold the buffer off the surface at a very slight angle, then turn it on and begin moving it slowly across the surface of the finish (see the photos on the facing page). Move the buffer about a foot every three to four seconds and work in sequence—edges first, then in toward the center. Work the buffer in smooth, confident strokes, and pay attention to the angle and rotation of the buffer when polishing edges: They may catch the pad and cause kickback.

The scratches from sanding disappear as you buff, and it's easy to see when you're done with the compound. Good overhead lighting or backlighting will highlight errant scratches. Follow the first compound with finer grits until you see a deep gloss appear. Let the compound dry, then wipe it off with a soft cloth.

At this point, some finishers apply a glaze that contains silicone or some other type of oil or polymer emulsion, which fills in the tiny hairline scratches. But I usually finish up with the #9 swirl remover—first with the buffer set on slow speed, then by hand. I apply a little to a soft cloth and polish the surface manually.

JEFF JEWITT restores furniture in Cleveland, Ohio, and is the author of *Taunton's Complete Illustrated Guide to Finishing* (2004).

Credits

The articles in this book appeared in the following issues of *Fine Woodworking*:

Photos: p. ii: by Anatole Burkin, © The Taunton Press, Inc.; p. v: by Mark Schofield, © The Taunton Press, Inc.; p.vi: (left) by Anatole Burkin, © The Taunton Press, Inc.; (right) by Mark Schofield, © The Taunton Press, Inc.; p. 1: (left) by Tom Begnal, © The Taunton Press, Inc.; (top right) by Mark Schofield, © The Taunton Press, Inc.; (bottom right) by Erika Marks, © The Taunton Press, Inc.; p. 2: (top) by Tom Begnal, © The Taunton Press, Inc.; (bottom) by Alec Waters, © The Taunton Press, Inc.; p. 3: (top) by Mark Schofield, © The Taunton Press, Inc.; (bottom left) by William Duckworth, © The Taunton Press, Inc.; (bottom right) by Mark Schofield, © The Taunton Press, Inc.

p. 4: Think Finish First by Jeff Jewitt, issue 141. Photos by Michael Pekovich, © The Taunton Press, Inc.

p. 14: Using Waterborne Finishes by Andy Charron, issue 125. Photos by Anatole Burkin, © The Taunton Press, Inc.

p. 22: New Water-Based Finishes by Andy Charron, issue 133. Photos by Anatole Burkin, © The Taunton Press, Inc.

p. 30: Tips for Better Sanding by Lon Schleining, issue 135. Photos by Matthew Teague, © The Taunton Press, Inc.

p. 38: Taking the Spray-Finish Plunge by Andy Charron, issue 113. Photos by staff, © The Taunton Press, Inc.

p. 42: Which Spray System is Right for You? by Chris A. Minick, issue 113. Photos by Alec Waters, © The Taunton Press, Inc.

p. 48: Turbine HVLP Sprayers Keep Getting Better by Chris A. Minick, issue 137. Photos by Michael Pekovich, © The Taunton Press, Inc. except photos on pp. 48 & 56 by William Duckworth, © The Taunton Press, Inc.

p. 58: Vacuum Motor Turns Into a Spray Rig by Nick Yinger, issue 106. Photos by Jonathan Binzen, © The Taunton Press, Inc.; Drawing by Heather Lambert, © The Taunton Press, Inc.

p. 64: Touch-Up Spray Guns by Jeff Jewitt, issue 154. Photos by William Duckworth, © The Taunton Press, Inc. except for photos on p. 64 and the bottom photo on p. 65 by Erika Marks, © The Taunton Press, Inc.

p. 67: TLC for Spray Guns by Andy Charron, issue 136. Photos by Anatole Burkin, © The Taunton Press, Inc.; Drawings by Bob La Pointe, © The Taunton Press, Inc.

p. 70: A Low-Cost Spray Booth by Jeff Jewitt, issue 139. Photos by William Duckworth, © The Taunton Press, Inc.

p. 74: Setting Up to Spray by Jeff Jewitt, issue 169. Photos by Mark Schofield, © The Taunton Press, Inc., except photo on p. 76 by Kelly J. Dunton, © The Taunton Press, Inc.; Drawings by Vince Babak, © The Taunton Press, Inc.

p. 78: Spray Basics by Jeff Jewitt, issue 169. Photos by Mark Schofield, © The Taunton Press, Inc.; Drawings by Vince Babak, © The Taunton Press, Inc.

p. 90: Spray Finishing Done Right by Andy Charron, issue 117. Photos by Alec Waters, © The Taunton Press, Inc., except photos on pp. 96 & 97 by Boyd Hagen, © The Taunton Press, Inc.

p. 98: All About Thinning Finishes by Jeff Jewitt, issue 151. Photos by Mark Schofield, © The Taunton Press, Inc., except photos on p. 100 (top), p. 101, 103, 105 & 107 by Erika Marks, © The Taunton Press, Inc.

p. 108. Aerosol Finishes by Chris A. Minick, issue 162. Photos by Mark Schofield, © The Taunton Press, Inc. except photos on p. 111 by Kelly J. Dunton, © The Taunton Press, Inc.; Drawings by Bob La Pointe, © The Taunton Press, Inc.

p. 115: Better Painted Furniture by Chris Minick, issue 111. Photos by Alec Waters, © The Taunton Press, Inc.

p. 121: Three Steps to a Flawless Painted Finish by Paul Snyder, issue 177. Photos by Mark Schofield, © The Taunton Press, Inc.

p. 130: Glazing With Polyurethane by M. David Becton, issue 147. Photos by Tom Begnal, © The Taunton Press, Inc.except for photos on p. 131 by Michael Pekovich, © The Taunton Press, Inc.

p. 138: Using Wood Bleach by Jeff Jewitt, issue 124. Photos by William Duckworth, © The Taunton Press, Inc.

p. 144: The Quick, Modern Way to a Polished Finish by Jeff Jewitt, issue 134. Photos by William Duckworth, © The Taunton Press, Inc., except top right photos on both pp. 145 & 146 by Michael Pekovich, © The Taunton Press, Inc.

Index

The New Best of Fine Woodworking series

A collection of the best articles from the last ten years of Fine Woodworking.

Designing Furniture
The New Best of Fine Woodworking
From the editors of FWW
ISBN 1-56158-684-6
Product #070767
$17.95 U.S. /$25.95 Canada

Working with Routers
The New Best of Fine Woodworking
From the editors of FWW
ISBN 1-56158-685-4
Product #070769
$17.95 U.S. /$25.95 Canada

Small Woodworking Shops
The New Best of Fine Woodworking
From the editors of FWW
ISBN 1-56158-686-2
Product #070768
$17.95 U.S. /$25.95 Canada

Designing and Building Cabinets
The New Best of Fine Woodworking
From the editors of FWW
ISBN 1-56158-732-X
Product #070792
$17.95 U.S. /$25.95 Canada

Building Small Projects
The New Best of Fine Woodworking
From the editors of FWW
ISBN 1-56158-730-3
Product #070791
$17.95 U.S. /$25.95 Canada

Traditional Finishing Techniques
The New Best of Fine Woodworking
From the editors of FWW
ISBN 1-56158-733-8
Product #070793
$17.95 U.S. /$25.95 Canada

Working with Handplanes
The New Best of Fine Woodworking
From the editors of FWW
ISBN 1-56158-748-6
Product #070810
$17.95 U.S. /$25.95 Canada

Workshop Machines
The New Best of Fine Woodworking
From the editors of FWW
ISBN 1-56158-765-6
Product #070826
$17.95 U.S. /$25.95 Canada

Working with Tablesaws
The New Best of Fine Woodworking
From the editors of FWW
ISBN 1-56158-749-4
Product #070811
$17.95 U.S. /$25.95 Canada

Selecting and Using Hand Tools
The New Best of Fine Woodworking
From the editors of FWW
ISBN 1-56158-783-4
Product #070840
$17.95 U.S. /$25.95 Canada

Traditional Projects
The New Best of Fine Woodworking
From the editors of FWW
ISBN 1-56158-784-2
Product #070839
$17.95 U.S. /$25.95 Canada

Workstations and Tool Storage
The New Best of Fine Woodworking
From the editors of FWW
ISBN 1-56158-785-0
Product #070838
$17.95 U.S. /$25.95 Canada

The New Best of Fine Woodworking Slipcase Set Volume 1

Designing Furniture
Working with Routers
Small Woodworking Shops
Designing and Building Cabinets
Building Small Projects
Traditional Finishing Techniques

From the editors of FWW
ISBN 1-56158-736-2
Product #070808
$85.00 U.S. /$120.00 Canada

The New Best of Fine Woodworking Slipcase Set Volume 2

Working with Handplanes
Workshop Machines
Working with Tablesaws
Selecting and Using Hand Tools
Traditional Projects
Workstations and Tool Storage

From the editors of FWW
ISBN 1-56158-747-8
Product #070809
$85.00 U.S. /$120.00 Canada